ISBN: 9781313405799

Published by:
HardPress Publishing
8345 NW 66TH ST #2561
MIAMI FL 33166-2626

Email: info@hardpress.net
Web: http://www.hardpress.net

THE GREAT COMPOSERS

THE
WORLD OF MUSIC

BY

ANNA, COMTESSE DE BRÉMONT

THE GREAT COMPOSERS

'In music dies poor human speech.'

New York

BRENTANO'S

LONDON, CHICAGO, PARIS, WASHINGTON

1892

PREFACE

IN endeavouring to compile these volumes, sacred to the memory of the dead, who, though fallen asleep, are living to-day in all the grandeur of their genius, I have approached a somewhat difficult task. I do so in all humbleness, feeling how little I am able to convey in words that which they have transmitted to posterity in their undying music. Still, in my poor endeavours, I may, perchance, bring some good to my fellow-mortals, by inducing them to contemplate the trials and struggles which these great musicians, singers, and composers have endured on their weary journey, buoyed up by the soul-inspiring strains of melody, battling against poverty and scepticism, yet loyally steadfast to their art. Perhaps, too, these pages may fall into

the hands of the loiterer through life, and
may arouse in him a hidden, inborn desire
to throw frivolity to the winds and to secure
a better and more lasting comfort.

What is it that has often soothed the
pillow of the dying? The strain of some
soft melody. What is it that has roused the
spirit of a forlorn hope to intensity when
charging upon death? The inspiring music
of a national air. What is it that checks the
wicked spirit of unholy men, jeering at religion and mocking God? The solemn tones
of the organ compelling solemnity as it
vibrates through the vaulted roof.

Then, too, the reading of these pages may
induce many an idle artist to strive in emula-
tion to rival those who have gone before; for,
though a hard taskmistress, Music is a rich
rewarder to all steadfast, conscientious, and
loving worshippers.

I am principally indebted in these volumes
for information to the works of Philipp Spitta,
Mr. Sutherland Edwards, and to the charming
memoir of Ole Bull, written by his wife,
Mrs. Sara C. Bull; and I have not refrained

in the latter case from quoting in her own sweet, pathetic words one of the most touching tributes paid to the dying master's last moments.

ANNA DE BRÉMONT
(*née Dunphy*).

CAVENDISH MANSIONS,
PORTLAND PLACE, LONDON.

"Music Washes away from the soul the dust of every day life."

Auerbach.

CONTENTS

	PAGE
AUBER : 1782-1871	I
BACH : 1685-1750 . . .	12
BEETHOVEN : 1770-1827	42
CHOPIN : 1809-1849	67
GLUCK : 1714-1787 . . .	87
HANDEL : 1685-1759 . . .	98
HAYDN : 1732-1809	112
MENDELSSOHN : 1809-1847	128
MEYERBEER : 1791-1864 . . .	146
MOZART : 1756-1791	157
ROSSINI : 1792-1868	190
SCHUBERT : 1797-1828	201
SCHUMANN : 1810-1856	218
WAGNER : 1813-1883	232

AUBER

1782-1871

THERE is great sweetness, mingled with dignity and reserve, in the face of Auber as seen in the portraits of the great French composer. The brow is broad and high. The eyes are deeply set, and seem to shine with kindliness through their half-closed lids. The nose, straight and prominent, proclaims the master to have been a man of resolution, although the sensitive curves of the nostril denote an emotional delicacy or timidity, a trait which is said to have amounted almost to a weakness in his youth, and the influence of which he never lost throughout the course of his long and eventful life. The chin, broad and strongly marked, bespeaks the convivial spirit and generous friend. But it is in the mouth we find the creator of melody. The lips seem attuned with silent song. A smile lurks in the corners with their witty curves. There is *esprit* in every mobile line. Altogether it is a charm-

A

ingly pleasing and at the same time powerful face.

Daniel Francis Esprit Auber was at once the greatest and the most characteristic of the French composers. His music has all the brightness and sweetness of his native land in its loveliest aspect, and again is full of the martial fire of that eminently warlike nation. The indescribable *verve* and *chic* of the French people are caught and imprisoned in his matchless melodies with an art that defies the inspiration of the poet and the brush of the most gifted painter.

The music of a nation is the voice of its instinct and taste, the language of its heart and soul. Art attracts all these, as a tree attracts the birds of the air. All seek shelter amid the fragrant shadow of her leaves. The poet soars from branch to branch, sunning himself on the topmost bough, or piercing with his golden beak the secrets of her mossy trunk. But music is a bird so *spirituel,* that its form is ever unseen as it flits around that wondrous tree. We can only hear its magic tones singing of love, of hope, of passion, and despair, of the homely joys of the fireside, of the stirring events of patriotism, and the divine aspirations of earth-bound hearts.

Therefore, greater than the poet, the writer, and the painter, is music. For, does it not plume its resplendent wings at the very throne of God Himself? What more fitting language could be chosen to express the spirit of a nation? Consequently, the man who is born with the gift to understand that secret voice can be the only true exponent of the soul of his people. Such a one was Auber.

In the year 1782 the master was born one bleak morning in January, while his mother was on a visit to the quaint little town of Caen. The Aubers were of old Norman stock, but a couple of generations born in Paris entitled the great composer to consider himself one ot her sons—a distinction he loved with all the ardour of a true Parisian. The Père Auber was passionately fond of music, and was himself an amateur of no mean pretension. Consequently, it can be readily imagined how happy the good father felt to discover in his young son signs of dawning musical talent, which, no doubt, to the paternal eyes assumed the proportions of budding genius. We can picture the refined and artistic home of the young Auber, before the vicissitudes of the king, whom his father served, brought trouble and disaster to that happy circle,—the evenings of song and music, when Père Auber taught the tiny hand of the baby composer to wield the bow and finger his beloved violin, when the gentle mother drew from the chords of her harp a wealth of melody, which awoke within the baby soul of her boy the first holy emotions of music. Can we not see the bright eyes sparkling with tears of joy, the chubby hands clapped with glee, until worn out with emotion the little fellow drops asleep, and is borne off to bed by the kind *bonne*? Ah! it was the influence of such simple happy hours as these that imbued the music of Auber with much of its pure and joyous character.

The master's youth was passed in what might be termed the *dolce far niente* of musical study. He loved to employ his time in writing pretty ballads for the delectation of the charming ladies of his mother's circle. And one of his songs, 'Bonjour,' had a brilliant if brief success. Finally, tired and disgusted with his failures, for his brain was not ripe enough to bring forth the fruit of his soul, he grew impatient with his musical fate, and resolved to devote himself to commerce. The good father, in despair, but still hopeful of the future of his son in the world of music, humoured the caprice of the youth, and procured him an engagement

in a commercial house in London. And subsequent events proved that the Père Auber was
as wise as he was tolerant of his son's vagaries;
for, soon wearying of the clerk's desk, the
master speedily returned to the crotchets and
quavers of his beloved song-writing. Inspired,
as he often declared, by the dazzling beauty
and exquisite delicacy of the fair English
women about him, he wrote enthusiastically,
and soon became a feature, if not a celebrity,
of London salons. It is pleasant to contemplate the debonair young Frenchman, with a
joyous spirit that rose above the damp and fog
of the chilly English climate, carrying the
sweetness of his song and buoyancy of humour
into the ofttimes depressing atmosphere of a
typical London drawing-room.

There is a story that one night Auber not
only lost his way, but lost his violin as well, in
a dense fog. Undaunted, he trudged along,
keeping up his courage by improvising a song
or two. At length he found himself near the
Thames. The faintly reflected glow of a
spluttering lamp, as the fog lightened, led him
to the welcome shelter of an inn.

On entering, the first thing that met his gaze
was the familiar sight of the green shagreen case
of his violin lying on the grimy counter of the bar.

'Mon Dieu!' he cried, as he seized the case, 'I have found you at last!'

'Wot's that daft little Frenchman a-doing with that fiddle?' growled one of a party of boatmen drinking at the bar. 'Take h'it away from 'im.'

'It's mine!' protested young Auber, as he clutched his prized violin.

'Drap it!' roared the fellow with an oath, as he struck out at the master.

But young Auber defended himself by adroitly avoiding the blows of the burly boatman, and shielding with his body the precious violin. At last one of the party of boatmen calmly observed —

'If h'it's 'isen, let's see if 'ee can play it.'

Now, in those days, fiddle-playing was looked upon by the ignorant as almost a black art. And the hostility of the rough crowd, assembled there in the dimly-lighted dingy bar-room, soon changed to a feeling of awe as they watched the young Frenchman, perched upon the counter, tuning his instrument. But when he struck the bow across the strings, and drew forth strains sweet and tender, awe melted into admiration.

'H'it's 'isen!' cried the burly boatman who had found the violin.

When the master was at last permitted to depart, he was worn out with playing for his insatiable audience.   The fog had lifted, and by the light of the early dawn the admiring boatmen led him out of the strange quarter into which he had strayed, and did not leave him until they had seen him safely under his own roof.

On his return to Paris, we find Auber again engrossed in the pleasant pursuit of his musical studies, dangling around drawing-rooms, at once the delight and the disappointment of the indulgent Père Auber, until at length what might be called the irony of fate decided his true career.   He had composed a concerto, but through a singular and inexplicable timidity dreaded to acknowledge the composition, and prevailed on his friend and *confrère*, Lamarre, to claim the authorship.   Success crowned this disclaimed effort, which was followed by another and still another, until the generous Lamarre finally disclosed the truth of the authorship, and young Auber found himself in a measure tasting the sweets of fame.   Soon we find the Père Auber, elated with the success of his beloved son, interviewing Cherubini on the subject, and seeking the approval of the great composer.

'My son!' exclaims the fond father, 'is he not a genius? See what he has already accomplished, and at his age, is it not wonderful?'

'Not a bit of a wonder,' abruptly replies the austere master, who had tasted all the bitterness of disappointment, and believed only in the sternest application to study. 'He knows nothing of music; tell him to sponge out all those little successes, and begin to study the A B C of his art.'

'Will you teach him?' anxiously inquires the Père Auber, a wise man, though an over-indulgent father.

'I will!' was the laconic reply.

And thus the life-work of the greatest of French composers began. There can be no doubt of the influence of the classic school of Cherubini on the inspiration of Auber, whose sparkling style, brilliant as a diamond, gained an added lustre in the pearl-like setting of the master's chaste and elegant method. Auber began no serious work until he was thirty-eight years old—an age which found Mozart and Rossini famous and resting on their laurels. But, as a recent writer wittily observes, he had the good sense to live to be eighty-nine, and thereby made up for the time which he had lost at the beginning of his life. Still, at the ripe age of thirty-eight, Fortune continued to play the wanton with him, and rewarded his first opera, *Le Séjour Militaire*, not with the fondly hoped-for success, but failure. Then he abandoned any further attempt for a period of six years. But the divine fire of inspiration could not be quenched by the mists of failure, and broke out anew, resulting in his second opera, *Le Testament ; ou les Billets-Doux.* Again the provoking jade Fortune deceived him, and brought him a second failure. But the fire of inspiration was not to be put out this time, for Auber had begun to believe in himself. He boldly attacked the fickle dame, and wrung from her a well-deserved success in the third opera, *La Bergère Châtelaine.* At this point of his career he met the man whose genius, combined with his own, was to bring them mutual fame and fortune,—Scribe, one of the most fertile of playwrights, and undoubtedly the greatest librettist of the nineteenth century. We can imagine the labour of love which these two great minds performed together. The delight of the writer to hear his words breathed forth in such divine strains, and the rapture of the composer on finding a mind whose language could interpret the wordless thought of his inspired melody. The fame of this artistic union culminated in Auber's masterpiece, *La Muette de Portici*, better known to the English-speaking people by the name of its greatest hero, *Masaniello*. Of this splendid opera, Wagner, that stern critic, whose judgment is undoubtedly as great as his transcendent genius, says, with a conviction thoroughly free from any undue partiality in the French master's favour—'*The bold effects of instrumentation, particularly in the treatment of the strings, the drastic grouping of the choral masses, which here for the first time take an important part in the action, are no less than original harmonies and happy strokes of dramatic characterisation.*'

This masterpiece was so imbued with the feeling of the time in which it was written— namely, the spirit of Revolution, which was fast arising to sweep over France, and crush the existing powers then reigning, as well as destroy all vestiges of the old *régime*, that it is said the performance of *Masaniello* was the flint that set alight the riotous fires of revolution in Brussels, whereby the Dutch were driven out of the country. When we realise the almost marvellous power of music in setting the hearts of men aflame throughout every epoch in the history of the world, we can understand the effect of this splendid opera on the spirit of a nation ripe and ready for war.

Strange to say, the death of Auber was due to the influence of those self-same passions he had so wonderful a power in arousing. It was the awful days and nights of the Paris Commune that cut off, in the midst of scenes of terror and bloodshed, the life of the charming debonair old master. And sadder still is the thought of the fate of all that remained of the dead composer. It is related that when his body was lying in the church awaiting burial, the mob seized it, cast it among their murdered victims, then, in their frenzy, set fire to the ghastly pile. And thus was lost, in the smoke of that tragedy of war, all that was earthly of the glorious intellect that had given to the world the soul-stirring music of *Masaniello*.

BACH

1685-1750

AS the Pyramid adds to the wonders of the East, so does Bach to the glories of music —a great monument looming up for all time. When the splendid works of a thousand musicians have crumbled, like the lost temples of Egypt, beneath the relentless sweep of ages, and lie buried in the sands of oblivion, the name of the divine master of Prelude, the creator of the beautiful mysteries of the Fugue, the genius of Counterpoint, shall live in those marvellous productions with a fame as enduring as the invincible walls of the mighty Pyramids. Colossal in their structure, heaven-born in their grandeur, pure as the stars of night in their spiritual simplicity, they proclaim the master to have been a true church-composer inspired by the most sacred feelings of religion, a man born of God.

'There is only one Bach!' exclaimed a famous warrior-king, and all the world of to-day echoes the eulogy of Frederick the Great.

Schumann, the sweetest singer of his time, and no doubt the most competent judge of the sublime works of the great master, laid at the feet of Bach this tribute worthy to be inscribed on the memorial of the greatest of mankind—

' To him music owes almost as great a debt as Religion owes to its Founder.'

Living ever within the shadow of the sanctuary, his life-work as *Maître de Chapelle* was bound by the sacred limits of the chancel. The altar was his stage, and the holy drama of the Christian faith his inspiration, which he poured forth in the grand, sonorous pæan of the organ, and voiced in the majestic measures of the chorale. He saw ever before him, with the eyes of the soul, the glory of eternity. Its wondrous light illumined with the glow of hope and fire of love the works which have made him the greatest and truest exponent of the music of the church. To his towering genius and intellect was wedded a heart as guileless as a little child, and a nature as simple as a peasant. Full of the tenderest family instincts, his home was his shrine, wherein he secluded himself, free from the ostentation, the hollow pleasures, and sordid ambition of a worldly life.

Germany has no brighter leaf in the glittering laurel wreath of her great sons than that which bears the name of Johann Sebastian Bach. The family of which he was a descendant was purely German, and could be traced to its home in Thuringia before the time of the Reformation. The earliest representative, we find, was Hans Bach of Gräfenrode, a sturdy peasant who worked in the mines of Ilmenau. Throughout the sixteenth and seventeenth centuries the name of Bach frequently appears in the annals of Gräfenrode. In the village of Rockhausen, not far from Arnstadt, dwelt, in the latter part of the sixteenth century, Wolf Bach, also a peasant, but blessed with considerable wealth. During the seventeenth century numerous members of the Bach family were to be found in the village of Molsdorf not far from Rockhausen. Above twenty members are recorded in the lapse of seventy years, the men bearing the names of Johann, Andreas, Georg, Ernst, Heinrich, Christian, Jakob, and Paul, many of which were constantly repeated in the line from which Sebastian Bach was descended. Johann Bach, who was musician to General Wrangel, was a native of this place, and the first musician of the Molsdorf line. He is quaintly described as 'an ingenious musician.' Johann Christoph, though a simple farmer, had a great reputation in his time as organist and composer in Thuringia. Near Gotha we find the home of the direct ancestry of Sebastian Bach. Through a labyrinthal pedigree, crossed and recrossed by innumerable Bachs, we come to Hans Bach of Wechmar, and his son, Veit Bach, the first of that great family of musicians whose strength, sweetness, and skill combined to yield to posterity the glorious gift of their last descendant. Like the wonderful plant that blooms but once a century, the hidden genius of a hundred Bachs blossomed forth in that one resplendent flower.

Veit Bach was a miller, and as his distinguished descendant says of him, ' He had his greatest pleasure in a small cithara, which he would take into the mill with him and play on it while the mill worked.' We can easily picture this homely music-loving man forgetting in the sweet strains of his lute the troublous times through which he had passed. Forced to fly from his home in Hungary, through religious persecution, he was driven from one place to another by the enemies of Lutheranism, until he found safety in his native village in Thuringia. We can fancy the placid, sunny life of Veit amid the whirring music of the mill, the melody of the dripping waters, the song of the flail as it swung to and fro, wielded by the vigorous hands of some lusty peasant. No doubt the steady rhythm of the wheel mingling with the sweet notes of his cithara made a sort of rude tempo to his rustic music, and thus taught him *time*. Can we not see the good peasant-folk, neighbours, and strangers, dropping in to the old mill for pleasure as well as business, to enjoy an hour or so of music when the bargain had been made for the wares of the musical miller? And thus was laid the foundation of that mighty family of musicians.

The art which Veit had so laboriously taught himself, albeit for pleasure, attained the dignity of a profession in his son, Hans Bach, the great-grandfather of Sebastian Bach. Hans developed a taste for music very young, and the good father decided on letting him become a *Spielmann*, placing him under the tutorship of the *Stadtpfeifer*, or town musician, who was also a Bach, doubtless a nephew or near relation of Veit, and called Caspar. The youthful Hans was soon ensconced in the family of Caspar in the tower of the Guildhall of Gotha, the official residence of Caspar. After serving his years of apprenticeship in this merry household where, owing to the near vicinity of the market-stalls, occupying the whole of the ground-floor below the tower, a homely German hospitality reigned—for the worthy farmers loved a little music over their pipes from Caspar and his pupils,—and where the pleasant duty of playing the chorale at stated hours, according to a quaint old custom, woke up the sleepy market-place, Hans returned to his native village, taking his place as professional musician together with the trade of carpet-weaver, and bringing to his fireside a wife, Anna Schmied, daughter of an innkeeper. To his skill as a 'fiddler' Hans united a merry, jovial disposition, and soon became extremely popular. His services were in constant demand to assist at the town-music of all the neighbouring villages. That he was a wit and a wag may be learned from a portrait of him, a wood-cut, in which he is represented playing the violin with a bell on his left shoulder. A verse supported by a scutcheon crowned with a fool's cap, declares him to have played 'in a way of his own,' and 'to wear a fine beard by which he was known.' From this merry musician down we find numerous Bachs, all doing honour to the family profession, some farmers and tradesmen, others holding responsible positions, but all serving God, as devout Christians, and their beloved

B

Germany through the many wars racking her peace and prosperity, until we come at last to the great master himself.

Johann Sebastian Bach was born in March 1685. The exact day is not known, although some of his biographers state the 21st of that month. However, the greatest of the German composers saw the light for the first time in the little village of Eisenach, at a period when Germany was still steeped in the lethargy of dejection, when the 'winter of discontent,' chilling her hopes and national energy, still hung over her, although the mists of frost and snow and ice were already preparing to depart beneath the approaching rays of the sun of prosperity. Like the first star of spring, the first flower of the frozen earth, Bach appeared, herald of the new and glorious season which was to pour into the lap of Germany such immortal blossoms as a Beethoven, a Handel, a Schumann, and a Schubert.

Before we enter into a few of the details of the master's career, let us indulge in a little psychological study of the ancestral influences which moulded the genius of the founder of the great German school of music. For centuries the family had lived in an atmosphere of music, earnest students of that divine art, amid the peaceful and picturesque scenes of the valley of Thuringia. Shut in from the outer world by its mountains, they passed their simple lives in the innocent enjoyments to be found in those rustic surroundings. Frugal in their tastes, healthy in their inclinations, rugged in body, they loved nature with an affection calm and deep, as devoid of passion as the air of those pleasant valleys was free from the taint of the great cities lying far beyond their mountain-barriers. The solitude of the fragrant woods, the sweet loneliness of the valley, the profound calm of the night, the grandeur of the storm tossing and surging through the mighty oaks, or dashing its way in torrents down the mountain-side, filled their souls with a poetic sense which found vent in music. For music alone could express their truly German appreciation of nature's beauties. Their metaphysical spirits sought within themselves the key-note to entone the sublime scenes before them. Their surroundings narrowed the outlook of their lives, but deepened and concentrated the feelings within them, until they became a spring from whence flowed the truest and most ideal form of music. The most primitive rustic of them all, would draw around him the good Frau and little ones, in the cool of the summer evening, or glow of the winter night, and call forth from his rude instrument sweet strains expressing love and peace ; or stirring notes depicting war and strife ; or again tink-ling, dance-inspiring themes, until the feet of his listeners re-echoed the rhythm.   They had not books, novels, or newspapers, neither had they the theatre nor the opera.   But they had the violin, the cithara, and the viol, all sufficient to them for the unknown amusements of the outer world.

As generations passed, each increased the store of musical skill handed down by their predecessors.   This wealth of musical legacy, tempered by a chaste and noble style, induced by the pious lives of all those austere Protes-tant men and women, brought to Sebastian Bach a heritage of music which gave to the world his transcendent genius.

At the age of ten years we find the young Sebastian left an orphan, and entrusted to the care of his elder brother Christoph.   The boy had been taught the violin by his father, Ambrosius, who soon discovered the little fellow's remarkable gift.   The elder brother undertook the course of musical training so abruptly discontinued by the death of his parents.   But this brother is said to have been a hard and austere taskmaster, and young Bach found the path of learning severely free from the kindly care and tender consideration of the lost father. Christoph, filled with the pride of seniority, endeavoured to quell the boy's ambition, which sought untiringly for more and more difficult pieces to master, by withholding from him some of his most cherished collections of manuscript. One, a work of organ music, excited the boy's desire to such a degree that he resolved to steal it from its place in the cupboard where Christoph had secreted it, thinking the boy would not discover it. But the eyes of young Bach, sharpened by zeal, detected the coveted scroll behind the wire network of the cupboard. And in the stillness of the night, when all were sleeping, the little fellow steals on tiptoe from his chamber in the garret of the old house, groping cautiously down the narrow stairway, through the silent room, until at last his tiny fingers find their way through the network of the closet, and he extracts the coveted roll of manuscript. With his treasure clasped to his breast the little fellow retraces his steps, now trembling with apprehension and dread lest that sleeping brother should suddenly appear like a ghost in the darkness. But the chamber under the eaves is at last gained in safety, and the boy spreads his treasure on the floor, where, by the light of the moon, streaming in the latticed window high above his head, he sets to work to copy the MS. The moon wanes and the dawn is approaching before his little fingers stop, worn out with their work, and he again steals adown the stairway to the bookcase, restores the treasure, and then scampers noiselessly back to bed. And thus every night for months this childish drama is enacted, until the boy has copied the entire work; but alas! that the work of all those patient nights should have been ruthlessly and heartlessly confiscated by that hard, unsympathetic brother. It is an old story, told by every biographer of Bach, in almost every language of the present day; but it is always pathetic, always teaching its lesson, that the parents and guardians of children may well take to heart,—the lesson that inculcates tender consideration in lieu of unreasoning severity with the innocent vagaries of child-hood.

The boyhood of Bach was sad and full of vicissitudes. After the death of his brother Christoph he was again thrown on the world. His beautiful soprano voice attracted the attention of the master of the St. Michael's

Gymnasium at Lüneburg. And he was soon installed as chorister in the local choir, and a place given him in the school, where he was trained in music and instructed in the general rudiments of a common education. Again misfortune overtook the poor lad in the loss of his voice. Then ensued a period of three long years of solitude and semi-starvation. Although a pupil at the school, he had no means of support, and lived as best he could ; but it has never been discovered how he earned money for his board and lodging. Still those dreary times had their solace in the boy's wonderful love of music and delight in nature. The long tramp of five German miles from Lüneburg to the town of Hamburg, where he went to hear the great Reinken play the organ of the Church of St. Katherine, was full of pleasure. Life was young within him, and he was filled with the intense capacity for enjoyment that sent his steps bounding along over the grassy fields, drove him into a merry chase after a flying squirrel, or tempted him into climbing a tree to take a peep at some feathered family in their nest. It sharpened the young appetite until the crusts of bread, eaten during a rest while stretched under the shade of an oak, tasted as sweet as the feast of a prince. And when the

town was reached another joy greeted the dusty
worn-out boy as he crept into a hiding-place
near the organ, from whence he could both see
and hear the great master at his post by the
instrument, totally unconscious of his secret
listener ; for Reinken was very jealous of his
art, and would permit no one to hear him
practise the methods which gave him proficiency in his playing.   And so the master
played hour after hour, ravishing the ears of
the boy with rich melody.   When darkness
had settled down on church and town, the poor
lad would set out on his long tramp back to
Lüneburg, weary of limb, but happy of heart,
his soul refreshed and strengthened by that
stolen feast of music.   However, the hour of
catastrophe at last came.   One summer day
young Bach more than usually worn out by his
journey from Lüneburg, footsore and hungry,
crept into his hiding-place in the organ loft.
The sweet strains evoked by the nimble fingers
of Reinken soothed him, making him forget the
long German miles, the hot, dusty road, the
hunger gnawing his empty stomach, until lulled
into a sleep he lost his balance and fell from
the narrow ledge of the organ on which he
crouched.   In surprise and rage the master
seized the luckless boy and gave him such a

vigorous cuffing that he fell almost fainting at his feet.   Then touched by the boy's pallid face he roughly asked him what he was doing there.

'I am hungry,' answered young Bach, turning his eyes towards the instrument.

'For what?' brusquely cried the master.

'For more music.'

But the master, angry and frightened at the boy's persistence, drove him off, and that was the end of young Bach's stolen concerts, although years after, when he had returned to Lüneburg a famous performer on that noble instrument, and the master was an old man of ninety-nine years, he embraced, with tears in his eyes, the man whom as a lad he had beaten and driven away, hailing him as his successor, worthy to wear his mantle as the master of improvisation.   Such is the irony of Fate.

Now and then, on those tramps in quest of music, Bach would meet with a helping friend, ofttimes a comrade as poor as himself, but for the time better equipped with refreshments; or a good-natured peasant would invite him to take a seat in the cart, regaling him with food and gossip.   Again Luck would suddenly smile on him, as it did one day when he was returning from Hamburg without a meal of any kind. Passing a wayside inn he paused before it, looking wistfully and longingly at its hospitable doors ; which, alas ! could not open for him, since he had not the wherewithal to buy a morsel of the cooking viands, the fragrance of which was so temptingly borne to him. He would not beg, poor, proud German lad ; but some kind heart within was touched by his appealing face, for when he turned to go a couple of herring-heads fell at his feet. He gladly picked them up, and pocketing them pursued his road homewards. The joy of the starving boy may easily be imagined when he found in each head a Danish ducat. No doubt the welcome gift cheered him with the thought of all the unseen, unknown benefits perhaps awaiting him in the future, as well as affording him two or three journeys to Hamburg.

At length the dismal record of school-days came to an end, and the boy's life began to put forth blossoms. He was soon appointed to a place as violinist in the court chapel of the Duke of Saxe-Weimar, a position he no doubt owed to the influence of his numerous relations in Saxony. Life at Weimar began very pleasantly and auspiciously for the young artist. The security of a position of independence,

however humble, gave him fresh interest in
his musical studies.   His training heretofore
had been on the organ and clavier playing.
Now he found near him opportunities of making
acquaintance with other branches of his art,
particularly with the Italian works which were
in great favour at the court.   Johann Paul·
Westhoff, the private musician of the Duke,
evinced much interest in the youthful Bach,
and no doubt aided him to a considerable
degree by his experience in music as well as
the world, for Westhoff was a man of much
culture and kindliness of heart.   Another influence in the art-life of the youth was the
renowned organist, Johann Effler, who kept
him in touch with church music, and assisted
to mature his innate gift for sacred music.
These and other minor interests served to
make Bach pass a few very happy months.
During the stay at Weimar he paid a visit
to Arnstadt, an old town filled with memories
of numerous Bachs, whose generations had
lived and died there, all pursuing their beloved
avocation of music.   Naturally the young
Sebastian's heart yearned to see the old place,
and he seized the first chance of paying it a
visit.   Now, a new organ had been recently
built in Arnstadt, and all that was needed to

make the Consistory happy was an organist of
skill and renown sufficient to do justice to the
post and the instrument, the pride of the town.
So we find young Bach almost stumbling into
the arms of his first real opportunity.   He
offered to play only for the love of the art
which made him the master of the noble
instrument.   The Consistory came to enjoy
the pleasure of hearing their fine organ played
by a young and ambitious stranger.   Their
curiosity soon turned to wonder and admiration, and they lost no time in securing Sebastian
at—for a poor musician—a very handsome
salary, partly contributed by the church, and
partly by the townsfolk.   We can imagine the
joy of Sebastian at thus finding himself suddenly installed as the master of a splendid
instrument, in that quaint old lovely town so full
of tender family associations, with duties comparatively light and any amount of leisure in
which to pursue his favourite studies.   What
divine ecstasy thrilled his whole being as
he heard the mellow golden music swelling
from the throat of the organ beneath the
touch of his hands, filling every corner of the
great church with heavenly sound!   It is said
that he would play the simplest hymn-tune
with such exquisite beauty that the congre-

gation forgot, in their reverent admiration, to sing.

Two years of peaceful life, passed between his duties and great study, brought Bach to a period in which he felt the need of fresh inspiration, the want of artistic intercourse with superior minds ; in fact, the fire of enthusiastic work had died out ; he realised the necessity of new fuel to feed the flame. A leave of absence was asked, and granted by the Consistory for the space of four weeks. With the money saved out of his salary he undertook the long journey on foot to Lübeck, a distance of fifty miles. His object was to see and hear the great master of Lübeck, Dietrich Buxtehude. With heroic patience Bach set out on this long tedious tramp at the end of autumn, in order to reach Lübeck in time for the celebrated *Abendmusiken*, or evening performances held in the Church of St. Mary's of Lübeck during Advent. These evening concerts had been instituted by Buxtehude at once for the edification and education of the people, and became an institution which lasted for two centuries.

The closing light of the short autumn day found the worn-out youth entering the cheery streets of Lübeck. The homely rays from inn and cottage greeted him kindly. A humble resting-place is soon found by the ambitious boy, who wisely resolved to expend sparingly his small store of savings in the poor and cleanly loft of a working man's cottage. A coarse but generous supper soon refreshed him, and in the soft autumn night, under the light of the full silvery moon, we see him set out on a lonely stroll through the sleeping town. We join him in his nocturnal wanderings until his steps linger beside the fine old church of St. Mary's, where he pauses to gaze with fond reverence on the sacred pile, to him the temple of music wherein slumbers the melodious soul of the great organ. We might almost feel the thoughts of his soul, swelling with . beautiful passion into the strains of a silent canticle of thanksgiving, as his eyes dwell on the abode, hushed in repose, of the great master he had journeyed so long and weariedly to see and hear. Perhaps as he pressed his cot, tears softened his hard pillow, tears of joy that he would awaken to find his dreams of the past two years at last realised. Simple German youth that he was, he possessed all the wonderful childlike depth of feeling of his nation, a marvellous spring of emotion that could make the strongest nature melt with sympathy, not with the actual fact alone, but the bare thought of the realisation of some cherished object.

The picture of the entrance of the unknown and friendless Bach into Lübeck would not be complete without the contrasting one of the entrance of his great contemporary Handel into the same town, alas, how different! Handel departs from Hamburg in the glorious weather of midsummer, his journey made delightful by the care and attentions of admiring friends, while his entrance into Lübeck is one of social and municipal rejoicing. For has he not come at the invitation of the Town-council to hear and try their grand organ, and accept a very handsome honorarium, should it suit his pleasure to remain in their midst for a time?

Buxtehude was not long in discovering the genius of the youth who so humbly and enthusiastically sought him out. And Bach soon found himself in a new sphere of art, which fascinated him to such a degree that he plunged into this fresh field of study with a zest that drove everything else out of his mind. We find the leave of absence lengthening from weeks to months, and Bach still lingering in that charmed influence. Buxtehude had brought the science of the organ to a stage of great development. His chorales were finely constructed, but lacked

the poetic treatment.   Herein Bach surpassed
him, as he did in everything he received from
the old master.   It is a most interesting study
in itself, this study of the style and methods of
Buxtehude and its influence on Bach, who,
while assimilating all these new methods, nevertheless left upon them the stamp of his own
peculiar genius.   On his return to Arnstadt,
Bach found himself involved in complications
with the Consistory.   They grumbled at his
long absence, brought him to task for neglect-
ing to *make music* with the scholars, or, in
other words, give singing lessons to the pupils
of the college attached to the church——a request
which Bach calmly ignored,——and last, but not
least, the quaint protest raised against ' the
stranger maiden ' whom he had allowed to show
herself and *make music* in the choir.   Here we
come to the first romance in the life of Bach.
The mystery of the stranger maiden was not
explained to the Consistory ; for Bach, tired of
the difficulties with that good body, which had
begun to embitter his position, resolved to leave
Arnstadt.   A year later, when installed as
organist at Mühlhausen, Bach began a new era
in his life by his marriage to the *stranger maiden.*
No doubt the gossiping old ladies of Arnstadt
were relieved when the news reached the little

town that the gifted young Bach had not fallen
a prey to any worldly siren, and all the pretty
courting carried on right under their noses in
the old choir-loft had resulted in the delightful
excitement of a wedding. The Consistory regretted their harshness, and would have the
young couple return, but Bach paid no heed
either to apologies or to renewed offers. The
marriage was recorded in the following quaint
and formal style :—'*On Oct. 17th, 1707, the
respectable Herr Johann Sebastian Bach, a
bachelor, and organist to the Church of Saint
Blasius at Mühlhausen, the surviving lawful son
of the late most respectable Herr Ambrosius Bach,
the famous town organist and musician of
Eisenach, was married to the virtuous maiden
Maria Barbara Bach, the youngest surviving
unmarried daughter of the late very respectable
and famous artist Herr Johann Michael Bach,
organist at Gehren, here in our house of God, by
the favour of our gracious ruler, after their banns
had been read in Arnstadt.*'

The bride was his cousin, therefore young
Bach followed the family tradition in marrying
a maiden of his own kin. The happy couple
set up housekeeping in comfortable style, enabled so to do by a legacy which happened
to fall to them quite opportunely through the

C

death of a brother of Sebastian's mother.   This
step endowed the young composer's position
with more dignity and security.   The happy
peace of a well-ordered home, the care of a
tender and adoring wife, the innocent delights
of family pleasures, and the sweet companionship of the little ones that grew up rapidly
around him, all combined to make the master
a perfect man, one truly patriarchal in tastes, to
whom the home was the be-all and end-all of
every hope and aspiration. When we consider
how essential the repose and seclusion of the
home is to the brain worker, especially the
musician, the poet, and writer, where they
may recuperate after the wearing flights of
imagination and drain of enthusiastic inspiration,
we can realise how blessed was Sebastian Bach
in the simple inclinations which found their
completeness and satisfaction in the domestic
circle.   Hence his great works, majestic in
their spirituality, God-like in their grandeur; for
they found their root in a life of godliness and
purity, the only true inspiration of enduring
fame.

From this period until his death the master's
career was one of ever-increasing perfection
and fame.   Antagonism did not daunt him nor
obstacles intimidate him.   He became the

honoured friend of kings and princes. Many
legends are told of the favour his genius found
with those great ones.   At one time the Crown
Prince Frederick, afterwards King of Sweden,
summoned him to Court in order to judge for
himself of the master's wonderful skill on the
organ.   Bach presented himself, a plain sober
figure indeed, amid the crowd of richly-clad
courtiers.   The Prince, with royal courtesy, con-
ducted the composer to his seat at the organ.
When the master had ceased a pedal solo, the
Prince was so carried away with enthusiasm
over the marvellous skill of his execution that
he drew from his finger a superb ring of jewels,
and with his own hand placed it on the finger
of Bach.   One of the courtiers in describing
the scene is said to have exclaimed—'His feet
flew over the pedal board as if they had wings,
the ponderous tones pierced the ear like a clap
of thunder, and if his feet earned him such a
gift, what would the Prince have given him had
he used his hands as well!'

On another occasion Bach was entreated by
a patriotic courtier to attend the Court at
Dresden and uphold the glory of German music
against French art, as displayed in the skill of
a Frenchman who had gained the favour of the
King by his playing.   Bach did not hesitate

to answer the summons, as the music of his
country was as sacred to him as its religion.
There may have been some political intrigue at
the root of the matter. But to the simple mind
of the master, thoroughly unsophisticated in the
ways of the world, the idea that the precedence
of German art was in question was sufficient to
fire him with zeal, and he set out with all possible haste to reach Dresden. The day appointed
for the contest which was to decide between
Marchand, the French musician, and Sebastian
Bach, the German composer, at last arrived.
The Court, in a flutter of excitement, had
assembled at the house of a great noble, whom
the King honoured with a special visit on this
occasion. When all the beauty and celebrity
of the Court was gathered together, the King
and Queen arrived and took their place in the
midst of the brilliant assembly. The French
musician, gorgeously arrayed in a velvet court-
dress, made his obeisance to His Majesty, and
then retired to an ante-room to avoid embar-
rassing his rival—so he declared. Bach, grave
and pale, attired in a simple dress of black,
guiltless of any ornament, advanced, holding
his plain three-cornered hat under his arm, and
saluted the King. The King glanced at him
coldly.

'So we have here a bold man who challenges the well-known skill of the Frenchman?'

'Even so, your Majesty,' replied Bach, 'but German art has no reason to dread French skill.'

'Oh! ho!' laughed the King, 'indeed, and is it as profitable?' glancing at the master's shabby dress.

'Not quite, your Majesty,' answered Bach unflinchingly. 'It aims at something higher than mere gain. It is not an art that tricks itself out gaudily to please the highest bidder.'

The King frowned at the noble candour of the master, while the Court listened aghast at the musician's frankness. Then the King exclaimed impatiently—

'Begin the contest.'

In silence the King awaited the coming of Marchand, whom a courtier had gone to fetch from the ante-room. The King still frowned and seemed in a very bad humour. At length the messenger returned and declared in breathless tones that the Frenchman had disappeared. A messenger was soon despatched to his lodgings; but on his return, he could give no tidings of the object of his search further than the news of his empty lodgings and the manuscript of a song dedicated to the King, which had been left behind by the absconding artist. Taking the book, the King bade Bach play, saying—

' Here we have the masterpiece of Marchand. That is enough for the contest. It shall decide.'

Bach seated himself at the harpsichord, playing not only the Frenchman's masterpiece with surpassing skill, but, taking up the theme, began improvising a fugue of such marvellous beauty that the King was overwhelmed with delight. His brusqueness changed to kindness. He sent the master away loaded with gifts, and honoured him by conferring on him the dignity of Court-musician and composer.

Bach's works are almost innumerable. He composed no less than three hundred and eighty cantatas for every Sunday and festival during five years. Many of these compositions have been lost, owing to the neglect which hung over his memory for almost a century after his death. Those were the busiest years of his life, for during the same period he wrote his magnificent Passion music, a work which will live as long as German music exists. Much of this splendid interpretation of the Gospels has also been lost. Only two remain : the one ' according to St. John,' and the other ' accord-

ing to St. Matthew.' The admirable custom
of the congregation taking part in the choral
singing during the services of Passion week
was, no doubt, the inspiration which incited
the master to set the sacred themes of the
Passion to music. He divided the story into
two parts, ending the first section with the
capture of Jesus and flight of his disciples.
The trial before Caiaphas, the denial of Peter,
the sentence of Pontius Pilate, the suicide of
Judas, the march to Calvary, the crucifixion,
death, and burial of Jesus—all occur in the
second part. The contrast in a theme of such
solemn grandeur and sacred woe required
workmanship of the most decided genius.
Bach has accomplished all this in his stupendous composition, which, had he never written
any other work, would have been sufficient to
immortalise his name. He has employed with
singular power a double chorus in the vehement
scenes of the mob pursuing and persecuting
Christ. Each sings singly until the climax is
reached, when they coalesce in a mighty burst
of passionate rage. The effect is as startling
as it is terrible in its *abandon*. The contrast
between the first part, with its solemn calm,
like the lull before a storm, and the second,
full of the clash of passion, thunder of rage,

and whirl of doom, is well-nigh indescribable.
The one is essentially lyric in form and the
other dramatic. The musical world owes to
Mendelssohn a debt of eternal gratitude for
his revival of this sublime work at Berlin exactly one century after its first production.
Since then the master has been studied and
played, to the infinite benefit of modern music.
No master of the fugue has ever arisen to inherit
the mantle of Bach. His fugues are as poetical
in theme as they are wonderful in construction,
while his preludes are mines of musical wealth
in the golden melodies lying concealed amid
their chords. Not to all, alas! is given the
power to penetrate their mysteries. It was the
genius of a Gounod alone that could have
created the incomparable melody of the *Ave
Maria* wedded to the first *Preludium.* May it
not be long ere another tone-poet shall ravish
our senses with a like discovery!

The last years of the great master were, like
those of his noble contemporary Handel, overshadowed by the cloud of blindness—a darkness that never lifted until the brightness of
eternity swept it away. He died the 30th day
of June 1750, surrounded by the few children
remaining of that band of twenty, and lovingly
tended by his second wife, Anna Magdalena.

The last thought of that great heart was for his beloved son Friedemann, to whom he left his precious work of the 'art of fugue.' And his last moment was a fitting close to that life of grand work, when he called in faltering tones to his son-in-law—

'Your pen, Altimiol.'

Then he began to feebly dictate to him the four-part chorale, 'If sunk in deepest misery.'

'That is the end of the art of fugue,' he whispered softly.

Then the flame went out, and nothing remained but ashes of the greatest composer emblazoned on the scroll of Germany's famous sons, Johann Sebastian Bach.

BEETHOVEN

1770-1827

IN the hierarchy of mythology there are many
gods—gods of war and peace and love.
In the elysian fields of music there are like-
wise many gods, among whom there is none
greater in the interpretation of human love—
none richer in expression of the deepest emotions of the soul—than Beethoven. Across his
work has been written in golden letters of
undying lustre the glorious name of Tone-Poet.
For has he not, in his flight to those heavenly
fields, bathed the wings of his inspiration in
the rainbow of sound? for sound has colour,
albeit invisible to human view, yet clear as
the rays of the stars of night to the eyes of
the soul. Has he not caught in every matchless strain the rosy hue of love, the dazzling
rays of passion, the sombre tints of despair, the
very blackness of death? In the *Moonlight
Sonata* he has bequeathed to us a tone-poem
matchless in the silver purity of its harmonies,

42

full of the mystical beauty of night in its dreamy voluptuousness, as it is full of the pathetic despair of hopeless love, which pervades its lovely themes like the purple mists overhanging a fair valley. How superb the colouring of the *Symphony Eroica*, fitting memorial of one whose career was the most splendid failure the world has ever beheld, whose light went down like some lost sun never to shine again—Napoleon Bonaparte.

Do not those stirring strains paint for us a picture of alternate light and darkness, sunshine and cloud? The thunder of the bass ushers in the storm of battle. The cymbals emit their crashing cries. Sharp as the clash of whizzing steel rings the whirr of the wind instruments. We see the smoke, we tremble beneath the shock of all this din of arms. Soon the tumult fades away. The low mellow note of the horns steals like the disc of the golden moon above the scene. The tremulous tones of the violins arise like dreams, soft, shadowy, unreal. In her mantle of peace Sleep has wrapped each weary soldier, like the warriors in Datielle's *Le Rêve*.

Again, what grandeur of tone, what wealth of purple colouring, befitting a royal mourning, we find in the *Marcia Funébre*. We hear the

plaintive introduction of the strings, summon-
ing up before us the pale face of woe.   The
heart-touching melody wailed by the oboe
reveals to us the spirits of the dead waving
their shadowy hands in mournful greeting to
the melancholy rhythm.   The sudden burst of
divine melody in the *intermezzo* comes like an
angelic song of hope, only to be drowned, lost,
extinguished in the sad wail of the minor, as
the last glimpse of the shore of Life fades for
ever amid the winds and waves of the river of
Death !

In the numbers of this impressive symphony
the genius of Beethoven has painted, with
touches of immortal beauty, the life of the
man who was at first to him the hero, then
the tyrant, despised and repudiated, but in
death restored to his place in the homage of
the great composer.

It was in the year 1798, when Vienna rang
with the fame of the brilliant deeds of the
first Consul, that Beethoven met Napoleon.
The master recognised his heroic soul, and in
his unbounded admiration resolved to erect a
monument in his own art to the Idol of the
time.   The personification of Liberty, who can
tell the joy of that labour of love ? and what
pen can depict the grief, the rage, the despair

of the master, when he found that his idol was not a god of gold, but a man of clay?

One morning the news was brought to him by a pupil that the Republic was overthrown, and its first Consul had accepted the Imperial crown. For a moment the master was dumb with astonishment and grief. Then the rage of disappointment overcame him. Snatching the unfinished score of the *Eroica* from the table, he dashed it on the floor, trampling it underfoot, while he cried in a voice choked with passion, 'Away with the tyrant! my hero is but mortal ; he has sold liberty for a bauble —away with the tyrant !'

It was years before Beethoven could bring himself to finish the work, for he was a Republican of the most ideal tendencies, and honestly despised kings and titles, thrones and empires. But the death of his fallen hero appeased the wrath of the master. He forgave his errors for the sake of that sad, lonely end on the rocky prison home of bleak sea-bound St. Helena.

'I have written the music to commemorate this occasion long ago,' he said, producing the score of the *Marcia Funébre*, when the news of Napoleon's death was conveyed to him. And then, after twenty-two years, was re-copied the title-page which had been destroyed that May morning, and under which was written with Beethoven's own hand, the legend—

  Geschrieben auf Beethoven.'

In the Ninth Symphony there is unrolled a sublime picture—a tone-poem whose immortal beauty soars to a climax of supremest ecstasy in the final hymn of joy. The spirits of Schiller and Beethoven are blended in that glorious unison of sound—

  Freude, schöner Götterfunken ! Götterfunken !'

Borne on the golden flood of human voices we behold a vision of Paradise itself, and, as they culminate in one mighty shout of melody, we seem to hear the angelic choirs re-echo the earthly hymn of joy.

The effect of this inspired hymn, one of the noblest interpretations of human yearning after the infinite joys of heaven, upon the vast audience assembled to hear it when first performed at Vienna in 1822 is described as electrical. Women sobbed, men rent the air with their shouts and embraced each other in their delight. The very performers wept. But all the while Beethoven stood at his conductor's post, silent, unheeding, like a motionless rock in that ocean of applause, until at last Fräulein Unger, one of the singers, her face streaming with tears, went to him and gently turned his face to the multitude. The master bowed calmly and then turned his back. Poor old master! cut off from the world by that terrible, impenetrable wall of deafness. The cheers and cries of those thousands of hearts thrilling with the wonderful beauty of his creation could never reach him. But what mind can ever fathom the well of joy and human love deep in that silent soul from whence sprang such heavenly music—for heavenly it may be justly called, since no echo of earthly sound had called it forth. That which is to ordinary mortals a bitter curse became to the master a blessing of incalculable power, a blessing in which the whole world has shared. As out of darkness cometh light, so out of silence came forth the sweetest concourse of sound the world has ever heard.

Beethoven had what might be called the beauty of ugliness, that is to say, the beauty of intellectual expression without the charm of feature which is supposed to constitute per-fection of face. We could not call a lion beautiful, and yet it is surpassingly grand in the pose of head and noble flow of mane. The master's was a purely leonine type in its square, heavy chin, firm-set mouth, broad, powerful nose, the small piercing, blue-grey eyes, with their gloomy upward look, shining like half-concealed fires beneath the heavy overhanging eyebrows from whence rose, grand as the summit of a mountain-peak, the noble brow crowned by clustering curling locks of steel-black hair. A glorious head which has been likened to that of a demoniac god by those who have seen him in one of his, alas! frequent, transports of rage. Again, when the master was moved by the enthusiasm of inspiration, that wonderful brow seemed to expand, the flashing eyes beneath dilating to a marvellous degree, while his diminutive body seemed to tower up as though filled with the gigantic spirit dominating that magnificent brain. At such moments he is said to have looked like Jupiter.

A pretty anecdote is recorded of the master's gallantry on hearing a lady compliment his brow. One evening while he was seated at the harpsichord in a crowded drawing-room, ravishing the ears of his listeners with his performance, a young lady, quite carried away with enthusiasm, expressed in very warm terms her admiration of Beethoven's glorious brow. The master overheard her, and, rising abruptly from the instrument, he advanced to her with a happy smile transforming his rugged face.

'Thank you, kind Fräulein, for your pretty compliment ; will you kiss my forehead?'

The young lady, who was *Maximiliane Brentano,* of Frankfort on the Main, to whom Beethoven afterwards dedicated his lovely Sonata in E Sharp, op. 109, arose blushing and smiling, and instantly imprinted a kiss on the master's brow.

The master was born at Bonn, the 17th of December 1770. His father, Johann Van Beethoven was a tenor singer in the Electoral Chapel. He died in 1792. The mother of Beethoven, Maria Magdalena Keverich, was a native of Coblentz. Of his grandfather, Ludwig Van Beethoven, a native of Maestricht, Beethoven retained a lively recollection. The old man had been a composer of operas as well as music-director and bass singer, and his operas were in great favour with the Elector, who had them produced with a degree of perfection quite magnificent for that period. During one of those performances, so the story goes, the old man picked up his grandson and placed him in the conductor's seat. The baby composer grasped the bâton quite stoutly in his little fingers, beating the time correctly, if vigorously, to the

D

great amusement of the Elector and the assembled court.

The master's first lessons were received from his father, who proved a stern task-master, despite his convivial habits. He kept the young Ludwig severely confined to his music-practice, a thing not easy to accomplish, for the boy was wild, restless, and headstrong, hating the long hours passed at the piano, as only a healthy, growing boy can do. He disliked equally the violin practice, and many were the devices to which he resorted in order to shirk the unpleasant duty. Shut up in a small chamber for hours with only his violin and the wooden stool on which he sat, the little Ludwig made friends with the very moths dancing in the shining sunbeams, and found amusement in frightening the mice scampering behind the wainscotting, attracted no doubt by the strains from his instrument, for mice are strangely susceptible to music. According to one account he found a rare boon-companion in a great black spider, who regularly appeared at the sound of a certain strain, and let itself down from the ceiling by its silken thread until it settled on the violin, where it remained spellbound by the vibrations of the instrument. The little Ludwig grew passionately fond of his queer guest, and when the spider kept him company never grew tired of practising. One day, unfortunately, his mother, on entering the room suddenly, discovered the great ugly insect, and, much alarmed, straightway destroyed it. The loss of the spider threw the boy into a fit of rage, in which he dashed the violin to the floor, shattering it to pieces. Beethoven never denied or affirmed this strange little story, although the recital of it always amused him greatly. ' For,' he is said to have once declared, ' it is much more likely that my horrid scraping would have driven the spider and flies away.'

For his mother the master entertained the deepest affection and tender memory. The report that he was a natural son of Frederick William II., King of Prussia, caused him great grief and vexation, and he left nothing undone to convince the world of the falseness of the statement. In a letter written by Moscheles, an intimate friend of Beethoven, at the composer's dictation, to Dr. Wegeler, he wishes ' *to make known to the world the unblemished character of his parents, and especially of his mother.*' This letter was published by Dr. Wegeler, together with a copy of Beethoven's baptismal register, thereby thoroughly refuting the fable.

At the age of sixteen the master began that

heroic battle with the world which never ended until the noble heart had ceased to beat. The good mother dead, the father banished to a small provincial town through his irregularities, young Ludwig was obliged to take upon his youthful shoulders the care of his two younger brothers,—a duty he worked unceasingly to fulfil, and not until that brotherly duty was entirely performed, and his brothers old enough to lift the burden from him, did he take up his studies as an artist. He became the pupil of Haydn, of Schenk, of Salieri, and of the master of counterpoint, Albrechtsberger. Close and enthusiastic study soon brought the master to a thorough understanding of his own powers. He felt within his soul the divine spring of inspiration, but he firmly denied himself the happiness of quaffing those sweet waters until the rigorous discipline of study had prepared him to derive strength, not intoxication, from them. Sometimes the genius within him would arise and thrust aside the conventionalities of study ; notably on one occasion when he had played before Mozart. It was their first meeting. Mozart seemed indifferently impressed with the piece. The master's pride was hurt. He eagerly asked Mozart to give him a theme. His request was granted with an impatience

almost amounting to contempt. Beethoven
began to improvise on the theme, playing with
such marvellous technique and beauty of expression that Mozart was lost in wonder. Calling some friends from an adjoining room, he
bade them listen, exclaiming, in the words
which have now become historic—

'This youth will some day make a noise in
the world.'

In those early days of his career the master
was obliged to give lessons, for the remunera-
tion gained thereby was no small assistance in
his straitened circumstances. But he detested
the giving of them, and rebelled against the
unhappy fate which compelled him to resort to
such irksome duties. It is told that he would
start out on a lesson-giving mission, but when
he arrived at the door of the pupil's house his
courage would disappear, and he would leave
an excuse 'that he could not give his lesson at
that time, he would give two the next day.'

It was at this period of his life that he first
experienced the consolations of womanly sympathy. The much despised teaching brought
him that blessing in the person of Frau von
Breuning, whose youngest son was his pupil.
This kindly keen-sighted woman at once per-
ceived the genius of the lonely uncared-for

youth, and devoted herself to the humane task of brightening his life, helping him by a thousand acts of encouragement and assistance, opening the doors of her home to him, where he found happiness in the society of her children. In a family of such refinement and culture the master could not but derive much benefit. There he became acquainted with the classics—the well-thumbed volumes of Homer and Plutarch became to him mines of richest intellectual treasure. He got a taste for French and Italian, and a knowledge of the poetry of his country. He would pass hours poring over Goethe. The influence of this worthy gentlewoman evoked in the breast of the youthful composer a reverent love, which was the foundation of his love for everything good and noble in womankind.

Soon the years of studious probation are passed, and we find the master the idol of music-loving Vienna. He has taken the place of Gluck, of Haydn, and Mozart. His compositions reflect the spirit of the times, the spirit of freedom and independence. He has given to the world the expression of those youthful aspirations in the wonderful *Sonate Pathétique*. In the words of Nohl :—' It expressed in full powerful tones what he himself

had lived, felt, and experienced, on the free
Rhine, and what had long slumbered in his
breast, till he had acquired the complete leisure
and outward security necessary for the pure
expression of his inner self.'

As the fairest summer day has its thunder and
showers, so was the golden sky of Beethoven's
inspiration ofttimes obscured by the clouds of
domestic trouble,—the vagaries of his brothers,
the sorrow and disappointment heaped upon
him by his graceless and ungrateful nephew, the
numb agony of unrequited love, and, last and
heaviest cross of all, the loss of his hearing.
He tells us of that awful affliction not only in
the priceless legacy of his numerous letters (in
one of which—the pathetic story of the flute—
he writes :—' I would put an end to my life,
only my art restrains me, and it is impossible to
leave the world before I have finished all I feel
capable of doing '), but in the wordless spirit-
language of his soul, the strains of his wondrous
symphonies.   It is in these we stand face to
face with the real Beethoven, revealed in all the
poetic grandeur of his true inner-self.   It is
not the deaf, half-blind, rugged old Beethoven,
wounded to the death by his misjudges, his
tormentors, and enemies.   No!   It is a Beethoven with the shining face of an archangel, the

glittering shield of a god, from which the sorrow, the pain, the bitter sufferings that assailed the human Beethoven fall away like spears cast against a wall of granite, from that guard of immortality.

The master had many friends, true, faithful, and sometimes adoring. Unlike Schubert, he never knew the remorseless grinding of poverty, the inevitable squandering of precious years in the work of producing mere 'pot-boilers.' But while accepting the various posts as music-master conferred on him by his royal or wealthy patrons, he preserved jealously the freedom of his art. He knew that music was a flower needing the full sweet breeze of liberty to nourish it into its highest perfection. The genius of Haydn and Mozart lost its bloom in the stifling over-heated atmosphere of the Court. The art of each was curbed by the caprice and pleasure of a royal master. Beethoven, like Bach, would never place the neck of his glorious muse beneath the foot of a king!

In accepting the patronage and friendship of Prince Lichnowski Beethoven was in reality the donor, for he enjoyed rest, quiet, and absolute freedom. The prince and his worthy spouse treated the great composer with a hospitality as delicate as it was deferential. They placed at his disposal a charming suite of rooms. The presence of the master brightened their childless home. The evenings were devoted to music, at which all that was most gifted in Viennese society assisted. Those were the happiest years of Beethoven's life, and those wonderful nights of song and music were like the planets streaming their light across the heavens above. It was on those charming occasions that some of the master's finest quartettes found birth. There in the gilded salon, aglow with the mellow candle-light, surrounded by beautiful women, their silken garments rustling harmoniously, their bright eyes resting adoringly on him, their gentle hearts beating to the rhythm of his creations, the master gathered his quartette—Schuppanzigh the first violin, Sina second violin, Weiss, Bratsche, viola, Kraft the elder alternating with Linke, violoncello—and poured into the souls of those gentle dames and gallant men the essence of his sublime muse.

Beethoven watched over the beloved members of this quartette with a more than fatherly solicitude ; he bound them to him by a chain of sympathy and pride,—sympathy as enthusiastic as it was genuine, and pride in being the first interpreters of those marvellous quartettes.

Moscheles records a letter addressed by the master to this quartette when, in 1825, one of his last difficult quartettes was to be performed for the first time before a select audience. It is quaintly humorous—no doubt the master strove to conceal his anxiety for the success of their efforts under the bantering tone.

'MY DEAR FRIENDS,—Herewith each of you will receive what belongs to him, and is hereby engaged, upon condition that each binds himself upon his honour to do his best to distinguish himself and to surpass the rest.

'This paper must be signed by each of those who have to co-operate in the affair in question.
'BEETHOVEN.'

(Here follow the four signatures.)

The master was a profound lover of the beautiful ; his love of flowers, and that fairest of human flowers, a lovely woman, was next to that of his passion for his sublime art. But Art remained his only mistress, his only bride ; whenever his heart wandered from her she drew him back with the leash of disappointment, and in her pure and tender breast he found consolation. For, truly, Art is a jealous love ; she will share her realm with none. Many and bitter were the poor master's experience ere he realised this.

Volumes could be written of Beethoven's love episodes, and the influence they had upon his work. His great heart yearned to love and be loved. Unlike Bach, he had no sweet domestic surroundings, no tender wifely sympathy. The homely joys of the fireside were to him unknown pleasures. It is a sad picture, that of the master's desolate home, uncared for, uncheered, at the pitiless mercy of unscrupulous, stupid servants, where disorder reigned supreme! After the rupture with his friend and patron, Prince Lichnowski, he left the palace and was a wanderer ever afterwards. Constantly changing his abode, the poor old master lived a life of squalor and privation, his servants bullying and robbing him to an incredible degree. On one occasion a valuable MS., the score of a mass, was missing, and after a long search it was found in the kitchen, where the cook had utilised the pages in wrapping up butter and such like edibles.

One day a friend found the composer sitting in his den breakfastless and fireless, nursing his face, which was scratched and torn cruelly. It was the work of a refractory servant. The friend promptly dressed the wounded face, and then proposed finding another servant.

'By all means,' said the master, gladly availing himself of the offer. 'But the new one must be steady, of good character, and,' with a humorous twinkle in his eye, 'not of a *blood-thirsty nature.*'

It is pleasant to turn from the contemplation of these disagreeable, pitiful pictures of the master's troubles to the delightful friendships, charming letters, and romantic experiences which go to make up the love episodes of the master's life. Dr. Wegeler tells us that Beethoven was always in love, and generally with some lady of high rank. Fräulein Jeanette d'Honrath, a beautiful girl with pale golden hair, a bright merry disposition, and a lovely voice, was his first love. She was a visitor to the Breuning family, to whose refining influence the master owed so much at that period of his lonely youth. His susceptible heart was immediately captured by the loveliness of this blonde goddess, and many were the musical offerings of song and improvisation he laid at her feet. He found a rival in his friend, young Stephen von Breuning. But the successful rival was one Carl Greth, a young Austrian officer, to whom she was afterwards married. A second affection sprang up in his heart for a pretty gentle girl, Fräulein von W. This little romance was a strictly musical love affair, and carried on through the medium of sweet sound. The young composer rarely spoke his love save through the voice of the instrument, near which the fair young girl would seat herself and drink in the secret message of his melodies. But these were innocent boyish rhapsodies, leaving on either side no sting of bitterness or regret. It is at Vienna that we find the master entering upon a serious love career; he is said to have always been in love with some one, 'making a conquest where many an Adonis would have found it difficult to gain a hearing.'

'Love is the feeder of music.' So the master has written; and in his case we may believe him, since many of his most exquisite masterpieces found their source in that wondrous spring, the spring of human love.

The first record of these loves of maturer years we find in a description of a picture of Psyche, in which Cupid is represented applying a torch to the wing of the goddess; underneath is written in the hand of Beethoven—

'A New Year's gift for the tantalising Countess Charlotte Brunswick,—From her friend, BEETHOVEN.'

Next we find him paying court to a beautiful singer, whom he had befriended in those boyish

years passed at Bonn.   Meeting her again in
Vienna, his heart is set aflame by her beauty,
wit, and genius, and the master lays at her
feet the noblest gift of man to woman, the offer
of his heart and name ; but the ambitious
singer rejects the poor composer,—'because he
is very ugly and half crazy,' she is reported as
having said when charged by her friends with
foolishly refusing the idol of the musical world.
But the master soon forgot the capricious
singer in the charming love-idyll between himself and the young Countess Giulietta Giuc-
ciardi, his pupil, who is described as being
extremely beautiful, with a lovely figure and
warm liquid-blue eyes.   Twenty years after
the master shows that he has not forgotten
the charming love of his youth.   In a letter to
a friend he writes of her—'*J'étais bien aimé
d'elle et plus que jamais son époux.*'   In a letter
to his unceasing confidant he reveals the sad
hopelessness of this love ever becoming a permanent one, yet rejoices in the solace it has
brought into his life, already shadowed with
that terrible affliction of deafness.

'Life has become brighter to me lately,' he
writes.   'I think you can have no idea how
sad, how desolate, my life has been—my deafness, like a spectre, appears before me every-

where. This change has been wrought by a dear fascinating girl whom I adore, and who loves me. After two years I bask again in the sunshine of happiness; for the first time I feel what a truly happy state marriage must be. She is not of my rank of life—were it otherwise I could not marry now, I must drag along valiantly. But for my deafness I should long ago have compassed half the world with my art—there exists for me no greater happiness than working at it.'

Unfortunately the charming young Countess was not permitted to bring consolation and happiness to her deaf lover for very long. A marriage was arranged by her family, which speedily put an end to this romantic attachment. Still she must have loved him tenderly, and felt the lack of courage which separated them deeply, for she is said to have sought him weeping, beseeching forgiveness for the act which had separated them, and we find the master consoling himself in the following reflection when alluding to the subject years after—'And if I had given up inborn inspirations for marriage, what would have become of my higher, better self?'

It is recorded that after the master's death, in a secret drawer of an old cabinet, amongst a number of letters, was found one containing two postscripts, which first revealed to the world the affectionate heart of the dead master, its sweetness and depth of sympathy, which his sonatas had already proclaimed in their rich beauty and tender pathos.. There was no name, no clue to whom these were written, but there can be no doubt that they were addressed to that early love—the Countess Giulietta—who surrendered back to him those precious letters, too fondly loved to be destroyed, and too sacred for a stranger's eye. We can picture the poor old master poring over each faded line in the long dreary after years, recalling in each sentence the sweetness of every emotion, living over again and again the joyous days of that happy past. Ah ! well can we understand—for who among us has not a like buried romance, a secret grave of love to which we often wander to keep green with our tears ?

There is another to whom the master paid the glorious tribute of his homage, long after that first unforgotten love—Fräulein Amalie Sebald, a lady of great gifts and distinguished appearance. But this was that strange love— love and yet not love, which is called Platonic, full of the sweetness of sympathy, the calm pleasure of intellectual companionship. The master has left a charming letter to this lady, the ending of which is a prose verse of quaint tenderness—

'Farewell, dear Amalie, if the moon shines this evening brighter to me than the daylight, it will show you the least of all men by himself,—Your friend, BEETHOVEN.'

In all that long array of beautiful women, clever and gifted, who were the subject of the master's immortal themes and inspiration, none stands out a fairer picture in her innocent devotion and gentle enthusiasm than the friend and worshipper of Goethe, the lovely artless child-woman—Bettina. In her letters to the great poet we read of that admiration for the deaf old master which stirred even his profound soul, absorbed in itself, to a keener appreciation of the marvellous genius of Beethoven. That the master appreciated the genuine sympathy of this charming woman, her wonderful touch with his noble mind, is proved by the passionate words found in one of his letters to her. 'Good God!' he writes, 'if it had been my lot to pass such a time with you as he [Goethe] did, depend upon it I should have produced many, many more great works!'

What more noble tribute from the pen of the

E

greatest genius the world has ever beheld to the power of woman to elevate as well as to inspire has ever been written ! And so let us leave the great tone-poet, with no thought of old age, no thought of death, but ever young in his transcendent genius amid that garden of lovely women, his friends, and his loves, like some brown nightingale singing in the pale moonlight to the sleeping flowers.

CHOPIN

1809-1849

WHO is this half buried in the shadows of a lofty salon—shadows a Whistler or a Lhermitte would have loved to paint—whose face, framed in masses of umber-tinted hair, and illumined by eyes of the same rich, warm hue, gleams like a cameo of palest ivory in the mellow light of the candles burning on the instrument before which he is seated ? The subdued rays flicker across the white fingers swiftly moving in and out of the bed of keys. The pale sensuously-modelled lips are parted in a smile of dreamy beauty—the delicate nostrils of the aquiline nose seem to curve more proudly to the measure of the music springing into life beneath the play of those slender, supple hands —across the white temples the blue veins swell and palpitate with the suppressed passion of those soul-reaching strains—the noble head s thrown back, while the full, round throat seems throbbing with the silent melody of his song.

It is Chopin! The very name is fragrant with the subtle charm of poetry, the essence of love and fascinating spell of mysticism.

Out of the shadows shine other faces. The marvellous eyes of George Sand sparkle like leaping flames beneath the burning glow of her lover's inspiration. Near her, in the fire-lit circle, looms up the grand, meditative, sphinx-like head of Liszt. Heine has dropped his glowering mask of cynicism; the soul of the poet smiles through his half-closed eyes. Meyerbeer with bowed head sits listening, his own masterly harmonies forgotten, led by the silver thread of melody through the graceful, light, fantastic labyrinth of Chopin's weird and beautiful conceptions. Ary Scheffer, pale as one of the classics of his own romantic school —Delacroix weaving a dream of colour from the tangled skein of brilliant chords and pale-hued modulations — Nourrit, the singer, his spiritual features aglow with chaste emotion— Mickiewicz, the great Polish poet, lost to view in the deepest of the purple shadows, where with closed eyes he revels in the poetic visions conjured up by the magic strains of his friend —Hiller, the man of the faithful heart—Baron von Stockhausen, ambassador and courtier, the devoted pupil. All that distinguished company is borne entranced upon the waves of melodious sound, mingling with the perfume of the hidden flowers; the rich reflections blurred and indistinct of the polished floor; the faint rustling of the silken curtains shutting off the world without. For Chopin is improvising. It is one of his weird fascinating odes to the night. A sonnet of dreamy mist-like colour and silvery vapoury sound—a nocturne. The soft frou-frou of the wind amid the trees, the drop of the rain, the sullen rumble of the approaching storm, the sweeping steelly flash of the lightning, the reverberating dirge of thunder now near, anon distant, more and more distant still, until it is swallowed up in silence. Soon is heard the sweet wail of the nightingale; she seems to shake the glistening storm-drops from her brown breast, as the wail is lost in a gush of melody soft and clear and tender as the light of the reappearing moon glimmering in the rain-dashed clouds beyond her.

And now, as the gushing strains fade and are murmuringly lost in new modulations, the lights on the piano are extinguished by the hand of one knowing well the player's moods and his love of improvising in the dark; only

the dull red gleam of the firelight casts wavering
shadows across the shining floor. A plaintive
melody, wild and sweet as the breeze singing
through the topmost boughs of a mountain fir,
steals into the shadows. It is a Polish air,
rising and falling with rhythmic tenderness on
the wings of memory from the dear and distant
Fatherland. At first it floats out dreamily,
yearningly through the room, then bursts
into passionate, pleading cadences, until every
bosom in that little assembly thrills with the
pent-up emotion of its moving refrain. It is,
they feel, the soul-cry of the composer as it
fades away in whispering chords low and pro-
longed, like clouds slowly sweeping adown a
distant view, and is gone.

Suddenly the silence is broken by a far-
away measure, grand, bold, and indescribably
thrilling ; louder and louder it grows, swelling
at last into sonorous, vibrating, martial rhythm,
filling the room with a rich music at once
melancholy and vivacious, spiritual and voluptuous. It is the Polonaise. And as the flashing strains surge to the stirring tempo, the
shadows of the room are alive with brilliant
figures dancing majestically to the ringing
echoes of the *Carabella*. Dames and knights
of the golden days of happy, prosperous

Poland, clad in gleaming brocades, shimmering
satins, silvery sables, stomacher and head-dress
sparkling with the scintillating light of clustering gems, and all the gorgeous display of the
Kontusz, they seem to the eyes of the listeners
to start into life, swaying and gliding, bowing
and turning in graceful rhythm to the harmonious measure. They see the sweep of each
cavalier's plumed and jewelled cap rend the
shadows like the flight of a dove. They hear
the faint rustle of each rich robe as its gentle
wearer returns with stately obeisance the salute
of the plumed and booted knight. Their pulses
quicken to the measured music growing fast
and faster still with each modulation, until at
last it bursts into a mad poem of motion, the
delicious *abandon*, the intoxicating, blinding
whirl of the Mazourka. Then out of the sudden
lull following that passionate climax, wanders
back like a lost spirit that same sad weird
Polish air, sobbing out its heart-touching melody
over the graves of buried hopes, the lost liberty
of that beloved unhappy Fatherland. With
tears and sighs they crowd round him as the
last strains die away. The lights are relit, and
with a smile in those beautiful eyes, bright with
unshed tears, Chopin turns to his little band of
worshippers, hiding with laughing words the
sorrowful yearning of his aching heart.

In the year 1787, when the capital of Poland was the scene of great political excitement over the election of the Diet, a young man who had just arrived was interested to such a degree by the activity of the picturesque old town that he determined to settle there. But the sun of peace and prosperity did not shine for long on the devoted city in which the young stranger had found a resting-place. Troublous times dawned on the unhappy country, and twice Nicholas Chopin sought to return to Lorraine, his native place. A strange fatality held him back, for on each occasion he was seized with a severe illness; to use his own words: 'It seems to be the will of Providence that I should remain in Poland, and I willingly submit. Providence had indeed reserved for him a blessing by detaining him in Poland, since, through his marriage with a Polish lady, Fräulein Justine Kryzanowska, he became the father of Frederic Chopin, poet-composer and pianist, whose genius has interpreted to the world the marvellous melodies and matchless dance-music of Poland.

Chopin was born at Zelazowa, on the estate of Count Skarbek, in whose house Nicholas Chopin was tutor. Music exercised a deep emotional influence over the boy from his infancy. So delicate was this inner sense that

a strain of melody would send the tears gushing to his eyes, and fill his childish bosom with
sobs.

'What grieves you, my Fritzchen?' the loving mother would anxiously inquire. 'Does
the music pain you?'

'No, maman; it makes me feel happy here,'
placing his little hand where he supposed his
heart to be.

This marvellous susceptibility soon revealed
to Nicholas Chopin the gift of his young son.
He placed the boy under Zwyny, whose teaching soon developed the latent talent of the little
Fritzchen. He began to improvise before he
had mastered the means of expressing his ideas
on paper, and we find him eagerly urging the
master to set the themes which flowed so easily
beneath his tiny fingers. In a few years the
boy's genius began to attract the attention of
the *dilettanti* of Warsaw, and we find him at
the age of nine years making his first public
appearance at a charity concert, quite carried
away with enthusiasm on this momentous occasion, an enthusiasm which was thoroughly
boyish, and busied itself more with the preparations for, than the artistic importance of,
the event. The little fellow's dress seemed to
engross his childish attention, for the good

mother had made up a handsome costume of blue velvet that delighted Fritzchen beyond measure, especially the collar, which was of rich lace—altogether a very gorgeous affair.

On his return from the concert, the mother, hiding her anxiety under a show of caresses, exclaimed—

'Which piece did the audience approve of the most, my Fritzchen?'

'Oh! I think they liked my collar best!' cried the little fellow naïvely, 'for every one looked at it.'

One day the boy was summoned to play at the private concert of a great lady. When he arrived, clad in the now indispensable velvet suit and famous collar, he became at once the centre of attraction to the crowd of beautifully robed ladies assembled, and was soon seated at the piano, his little fingers busily at work in improvisation. It may have been the gracious presence of all those lovely women, or the elegance of his surroundings, which pleased the boy's artistic sense of colour, but he played with an inspiration that surprised his mother, standing near him, and filled all with wonder and admiration.

When he had ceased, a charming woman, clad in a rich robe of crimson *moiré*, approached him. Clasping the boy in her arms, and imprinting a kiss on his forehead, she exclaimed—

'You are truly a poet, my little man!'

It was Madame Catalani, the great singer. Fritzchen passed many happy hours with the distinguished artist, one moment lost in childish admiration over her splendid jewels and gorgeous raiment, the next weeping with joy over the exquisite melody of her wonderful voice. And the height of his delight was reached when the kind-hearted singer presented him with a beautiful gold watch bearing the legend— '*Donné par Madame Catalani à Frédéric Chopin âgé de dix ans,*' as a souvenir on her departure from Warsaw.

The first patron of little Frederic was the Princess Lowicka, a gracious and beautiful but unhappy lady, who sought in art the consolations denied her in an uncongenial marriage. The young virtuoso was constantly at the palace. The Grand Duke, who was of a morose and passionate nature, shared with his wife in the admiration aroused by the boy's genius. On one occasion, while improvising, his head cast back and the beautiful eyes gazing upward with a rapt expression, the Grand Duke approached the piano.

'Why do you always look at the ceiling?'

he exclaimed brusquely. ' Do you see the notes up there ? '

To this curious speech the boy vouchsafed no answer, so absorbed was he in interpreting his inspiration, while the Grand Duke, whose word was law, and whose frown a thing to be dreaded, turned away smiling indulgently. On another occasion the little virtuoso demanded to have all the candles extinguished, a whim the Princess graciously humoured by putting out the lights near him with her own hand. But it was only when under the spell of his improvisation that he became a capricious young autocrat, otherwise he was as playful and childlike as any of his less gifted companions.

A great love of acting marked those boyish years of the great composer. Albert Piasecki, a famous actor of that time, predicted for him a future, and strongly urged upon Nicholas Chopin the wisdom of training his son for a histrionic career. ' Your son,' he declared, ' has every gift necessary to make a great actor. He has presence of mind, a charming facility of declamation, and a wonderful capacity for facial expression.' All of which is not surprising when we consider how near akin are the dramatic and the musical art. The one speaks to the eye, the other to the ear, while both depend on the same scheme of construction—plot, counter-plot, and climax. Out of that vivid inner sense called imagination, Chopin wove musical dramas of such rare beauty and quaint originality that he has become the Romancist of Music, the Prince of Improvisatores, the Regenerator of that much abused and little understood instrument the Piano.

The youth of Chopin cannot be passed over without a word of reminiscence about his sister Emilie. These two charming children, for they were nothing more, were a constant source of inspiration one to the other. Emilie had a wonderful gift for verse, and, had she lived, would undoubtedly have shared if not surpassed her brother's fame. She was five years younger than Frederic, and is described as bearing a striking resemblance to her brother. She had the same fair silken hair, the same beautiful eyes, full of tenderness and melancholy, the same exquisite sensibility, the same alternations of sadness and gaiety. These two wrote many clever plays in collaboration, which they performed for the amusement of the pupils of their father's school. They also founded a literary society, of which Frederic was the president and Emilie the secretary. We cannot imagine anything more charming than this childish symposium of art. Alas that it was destined to end so suddenly, through the death of Emilie when in the first bloom of early girlhood, at the age of fourteen years!

Among the cherished memorials of Chopin's youth, collected by the family, are two numbers of a little journal entitled *Kuryer Szafarski*, the editing and printing of which afforded the young composer amusement during his rusticating at a little country town. In one appears the following record, which speaks for itself in regard to the humour of Chopin :—

'On July 15th, M. Pichou [a name Frederic assumed] appeared at the musical assembly at Szafarnia, at which were present several persons, big and little. He played Kalkbrenner's concerto, but this did not produce such a *furore*, especially among the youthful hearers, as the song which the same gentleman rendered.'

About the same time, it appears, there was a number of Jews in the town for the purpose of buying grain. Chopin sent them an invitation to hear him play. The Jews gladly accepted the courtesy of the kind-hearted youth, and assembled in a goodly number. Chopin played for them a Jewish wedding-march, called *Majufes*, which so delighted them that they straightway began to dance and sing in their delight. They begged him to assist at an approaching Jewish wedding, and to play some more of his wonderful music. On the composer accepting the invitation, they departed, loud in their praises, and exclaiming gleefully, 'He plays like a born Jew!' Another interesting story of his boyhood is that told by one of his father's pupils. One day, it seems, when Professor Chopin was absent, there was a great uproar in the school. The master presiding was at his wits' end, when Frederic entered the schoolroom. Without a word of reproof, he requested the roisterers to sit down, called to those who were making a noise outside, and promised to improvise a story on the piano if they would be quiet. Instantly all was still, and Frederic sat down to the instrument and extinguished the lights. He described how robbers approached a house, mounted by ladders to the windows, but were frightened away by a noise within. Immediately they fled on the wings of the wind into a deep dark wood, where they fell asleep under the starlit sky. Then he played more and more softly, as if trying to lull children to rest, till he found that the boys had really fallen asleep. Presently he stole noiselessly away and brought the family with lights to see the slumbering children. Then, laughing softly, Frederic sat down to the piano and struck a loud chord. Whereupon the children awoke, and all trooped off to supper, laughing merrily over the musical joke.

Thus the boyhood and youth of Chopin passed happily along, like the placid waters of a silver stream purling melodiously through mossy banks and sunny scenes. Tradition is rich in anecdotes of those early years, and, no doubt, like all traditions, more fascinating for the halo of romance surrounding these records. There are stories of the young composer's wit, his boyish pranks and childish attachments, but none more characteristic than the following.

While travelling with a friend through the wastes of Poland they found themselves suddenly snowbound; a huge drift had swept across their path, and, but for the timely aid of some peasants, our young composer would have been lost to fame. But, with the help of some sturdy peasants, they managed, not without trouble, to reach the little town of Güllichan, where they were detained for horses. Finding the time hang heavy on his hands Frederic was agreeably surprised to find a piano in a room adjoining the combined kitchen and dining-room. Going up to it he struck a few chords, and then cried out in delight—

 'Santa Cecilia, the piano is in tune!'

Seating himself, he was soon oblivious of his surroundings in the dream of improvisation. Soon the music attracted the peasants, who came and stood behind the player, who called out to his friend, 'Now we shall see whether my listeners are lovers of music or not,' and began his fantasia on Polish songs.

The love of song characterises the Slav above all races. The rudest peasant might be lured to the end of the world by one of his national songs. Poetical perception and sensibility to the beauties of nature are eminently innate in the Polish character. The peasants stood petrified, captivated by the music so new and bewitching, their eyes mechanically following every movement of the pianist's delicate hand ; even the pipes, most important of objects, had ceased to be of interest to their owners and languished smokeless between the half distended lips ; the crowd increased until well-nigh half the population were gathered around the small unpretentious house, unheeded by the performer, who played in deep abstraction drinking in the creations of his own fancy.

F

At last the postmaster appeared. 'The horses are ready!' were the words which recalled Frederic from dreamland to reality. He sprang up. 'Finish that beautiful piece!' is the chorus of a dozen of voices. He looked at his watch; too much time had been lost already; his thoughts were expressed in his face. 'I'll give you courier, horses, everything that you want; only remain a little while!' urged the postmaster. Long afterwards, when the composer held spell-bound the critics of Paris, most fastidious of all publics, he recollected with pleasure the touching tribute to his skill by the population of this unpretentious hamlet.

Soon the gay life of Vienna absorbed his whole attention. Like all composers he was most anxious to secure the suffrages of the music-loving *Kaiserstadt.* His letters are full of descriptive incident connected with his appearance at the Imperial Opera House, and the anxiety which naturally filled his mind at so perilous an undertaking. But the result was all that could be desired, and he was much lauded for his performance of one of Beethoven's overtures, followed by his own variations and a cracovienne which is said to have occasioned an improvised dance on the benches by a portion

of the audience.   The latter part of his stay at
Vienna was dimmed by the ill-starred revolt of
his native country against Russian oppression,
and the terrible punishment meted out by
the victorious oppressors.   He had ever preserved a deep-felt love for the land of his
birth, and even on his deathbed his wishes
wafted   eastward   towards   the   wide   plains
and their inmates, sighing under an alien
yoke.

When leaving Warsaw a banquet was given
in his honour, and the presentation of a silver
goblet filled with Polish earth brought the tears
to his eye.   'May you never forget the fatherland ; think of Poland ; think of your friends
who are proud to call you their compatriot, who
expect great things of you !'   With these
prayers and wishes ringing in his ears he left
Poland, alas ! never to return.

Irresistibly he was drawn to Paris.   That
most elegant of cities was best suited to the
development of his graceful, zephyr-like genius.
Paris swarmed with his exiled countrymen,
and to one of them he owed his sudden and
unparalleled success.   Friendless and poor,
he despaired of his future, when a meeting
with Prince Radziwill and an introduction to
Baron James de Rothschild transformed him

into the lion of the hour, petted and spoiled by
the most brilliant society.

It was at this period of his career that Chopin
first met the gifted woman who was destined
to exert a powerful and fascinating influence
over his art.   One evening while improvising one
of his favourite themes before a delighted audience in one of the most brilliant and exclusive
salons of the Faubourg St. Germain, a lady,
remarkable at once for the plainness of her face
and wonderful beauty of her eyes, was presented by the Abbé Liszt, on whose arm she
was leaning.   The lady was George Sand.
On both sides it was love at first sight, a love
partaking more of the senses than of the soul,
for, as the composer afterwards wrote, the soft
rustle of her silken gown, the faint odour of
violets hovering round her, the deep tones of
her rich voice, filled him with an overpowering
thrill of sensuous pleasure, that was almost re-
pellent to one whose spirit had been chastened
by a most unhappy love affair.

He was irresistibly drawn to the feet of this
siren of the pen by the sympathy of intellect,
and a fancied resemblance to the object of his
recent attachment, a beautiful young Polish
woman of rank who loved him in return, but
not with a devotion strong enough to brave

the opposition of her parents in view of the difference in rank of the young composer. With a heart crushed and wrung with disappointed hopes, Chopin abandoned himself body and soul to the spell of this literary enchantress.

Months of bliss and years of gradual estrangement preceded the last act in that wild love drama, and the image of his lost Polish love, long forgotten in the affection of the most accomplished and famous woman of Parisian society, came back to him in increased strength as the bonds between them loosened. Proud to the last, Chopin rejected a love which he felt to be based on pitiful commiseration of his enfeebled health. The happy days spent at Majorca were henceforth to be only a reminiscence. The delighted admirers of many of his Nocturnes and Impromptus little know the pain and agony, mental and physical, which shadowed the cradle of those cherished children of his brain.

The last day was not distant. The Countess Potocka cheered his parting moments. 'Sing to me!' exclaims the dying man with failing voice. Choked with tears, she entoned Stradella's hymn to the Virgin, filling the room with its matchless beauty. 'Oh! how beautiful! how beautiful!' he mutters, in dying ecstasy.

When the last agony was impending, he whispered, 'Who is near me?' They were his last words. His sister and faithful friend Gutenann clasped his hands. Just as the bells of Paris chimed three, with the last stroke he sighed and all was at an end.

Flowers hid his grave, and the Polish earth, carefully preserved in its silver receptacle, mingled with its soil. His heart, restored to his fatherland, found an honoured resting-place in the Church of the Sacred Cross at Warsaw, while his remains were entombed in the Père Lachaise, beside the ashes of Bellini.

GLUCK

1714-1787

A VISION of loveliness in powder and patches, pouting lips and smiling eyes, enframed by towering masses of snowy tresses, flits across the page conjured up by the magical name of Gluck.

It is the face of a beautiful ill-fated Queen whose enthusiastic love of music bestowed on the great composer a royal favour which fostered and protected his genius. Interwoven with the superb harmonies and delicious melodies of *Iphigenia* are memories of the incomparable Marie Antoinette, graceful and beautiful, the very queen-butterfly in that garden of pleasure, the court life of Versailles, to whom Gluck offered the purest incense of homage, the simple gratitude of an honest German heart.

And to that lovely Queen, brave in misfortune as she was gaily frivolous in prosperity, the musical world owes a debt of imperishable gratitude for her discovery of the eighteenth century Wagner.

The name of eighteenth century Wagner can descend on no worthier shoulders.   Before his powerful mind asserted its sway, the operatic stage, steeped in antiquated Italian traditions, was tottering towards morbid decay.   Wherever the student casts his eye during the pre-reformation era of music, which included fully one half of Gluck's own lifetime, he is confronted by inane and trivial melody hardly discernible amid a plethora of senseless vocal gymnastics, calculated to display the singer's skill, with an utter disregard of the legitimate claims of plot and libretto.

The practical and manly mind of Gluck was the first to vindicate for the written test of opera that importance which alone can justify the co-existence of written words in contradistinction to purely instrumental works.   In the mighty era of musical upheaval which revolutionised the art in its very foundations, the important part so ably performed by Gluck, though acknowledged during his lifetime, has come to be somewhat unjustly overlooked after his death.   In his native country, Austria, his radical measures never met with full approbation, and France, the country which was the first to do him justice, was soon afterwards in the throes of political convulsions which dead-

ened for many years to come all musical germs,
while the period of lassitude which naturally
followed on a lustrum of unexampled stir and
feverish energy heralded in a revival of Italian
music, with many of the faults against which
the German master had waged a successful
warfare.

But true merit, though for a time it may be
obscured, must eventually assert its rights, and
it has been reserved to our time to vindicate the
master's fame by a revival of his *Orfeo*, which
will, no doubt, be followed by the presentation
of other compositions. The splendid reception
of this opera is a matter of recent history. It
has more than justified the courageous policy
of the theatrical manager. No better passport
to the older master's claims to be ranked with
the foremost exponents of his art could be
imagined than the enthusiastic plaudits of a
public familiar with the dulcet strains of Mozart,
Gounod, Wagner. And can the constantly
growing Wagnerite school do otherwise than
venerate the memory of one who, alone and
unaided, unfurled the banner of equal rights for
all component parts of opera, and placed music
above its exponent, nearly a century in advance
of their idol ?

He has expressed his views of the relation

between composer and librettist, in regard to
the production of opera, in unmistakeable terms:
to second the poetry, and in this combination
to elevate the soul.   It was the fashion to write
music for the vocalist, and to suit the capacity
of the latter for a certain species of gymnastics
at the expense, not only of the poetry, but of
the scenes exhibited on the stage.   In the
dedication of *Alceste* to the Grand Duke of
Tuscany, Gluck says, with a modesty which dis-
arms criticism: ' I shall try to reduce music to
its real function ' (*i.e.* in opera), ' that of second-
ing poetry by intensifying the expression of
sentiments and the interest of situations, without interrupting the action by needless ornament.'

This independence of character, as applied
to authority in music, was also exemplified in
Gluck's personal relations with great person-
ages.   A story is told, on the authority of Mr.
Sutherland Edwards, of a certain rehearsal of
Orfée, which took place in Sophie Arnould's
apartment.   The singers were all seated, and
while the *prima donna* was in the midst of an
aria, the Prince d'Hennin entered the room.
This ' prince of dwarfs '—as he was styled—
thereupon interrupted the proceedings, and,
addressing Gluck in austere tones, said: ' I be-

lieve it is the custom in France to rise when
any one enters a room, especially if he be a
person of some consideration.' It is easy to
imagine the blaze of indignant fury in the eyes
of the master as he replied : ' The custom in
Germany, sir, is to rise only to those we esteem ;'
then, turning to the intimidated Sophie, he
added : ' I perceive, mademoiselle, that you
are not mistress in your own house. I leave
you, and shall not .set foot here again.' The
Queen heard of the offence given by d'Hennin,
and insisted upon due reparation being made
to Gluck, to whom the Prince apologised.

Rugged and harsh the features of Gluck look
down out of his numerous portraits. To seek
a comparison we must conjure up the repulsive
grandeur of Mirabeau and Danton ; in vain do
we look for the placid gentleness of Haydn,
or the melancholy beauty of Mozart, in the
wrinkled countenance, scarred and seamed by
the ravages of small-pox, encircled by mighty
wig and illumined by a pair of eyes worthy of
thunderbolt-wielding Jupiter. But, happily, as
Victor Hugo sang, 'the *Heart* has no wrinkles.'
Gluck was afflicted with a violent temper,
which flamed up in lightning haste and sub-
sided as quickly into his natural goodness of
heart. Though his lines were cast in the

palaces of the rich, he disdained the wiles of a courtier, and in the behests of his art all were equal before him.

He knew not the bitterness of struggling poverty. The Empress Maria Theresa was his gracious patroness, and what higher honour could be conceived than the title of court composer and teacher to the Archduchesses of that Imperial court which honoured itself by doing homage to genius.

He was not exactly an ideal teacher, that impatient thunderer who hardly relished the task of supervising mediocrity, though it might be of royal descent. Full well can we believe that he lost his temper with the charming but wayward Marie Antoinette, and apostrophised 'her confounded Imperial fourth finger' which persisted in playing the wrong key. Honour alike to the sterling qualities of the old man to whom his profession was above rank, and to the amiability of the pupil whose unwavering attachment proved his mainstay against envious antagonists during her short day of power in gay Versailles.

The early days of Gluck were not remarkable; though undoubtedly gifted, his talents had none of that precocity so frequent in that age. A good musical education and fair ability as a violoncellist secured him an appointment with Prince Melzi, a nobleman of Milan, and his first successes were achieved as a thorough partisan of the Italian style. *Artaserses, Ipermnestra, Demetrio* are some of his early operas, performed in Milan in 1741 and 1742, which he was the first to condemn in after years. Two operas written for the Haymarket Theatre, London, achieved very moderate success, and were roundly condemned by Handel, who pronounced them 'detestable, and hardly worthy of his cook.'

This adverse criticism impelled him to cast off the shackles of the old school, and his next operas, *Alceste, Paris and Helena,* and *Orfeo,* prove that he had ventured on hitherto un-trodden ground. The Viennese, headed by the influential authorities Hasse and Metastasio, broke out in open revolt, and though Gluck's fame stood too high to be obscured, a partial recognition, such as he received, could not satisfy his nature, which was nothing if not thorough. With a perspicacity which is truly remarkable, he hit upon Paris as the soil most congenial for the propagation of his principles. Though well advanced in years, being sixty when he left Vienna, he took up the fight with all the ardour of a youth.

Nor could he have spared any of his vigour. The worship of Lully, Piccini, and Sacchini was in full bloom, and to challenge these tried composers was considered an act of temerity bordering on madness. True, Gluck had the support of the young Queen, but Piccini was not without powerful friends, and the whole influence of the court had to be invoked to counterbalance the intrigues which were openly indulged in with the avowed purpose to wreck the performances of the German master's music.

But *Orfeo* held the audience spellbound, and after its continual run for forty-nine nights, the performance of Racine's *Iphigenia in Aulis* effectually disposed of the pretensions of the Piccini faction. The star of Gluck, already in the ascendant, shone in solitary grandeur never to wane during his lifetime. The successive performances of *Iphigenia in Tauris, Armida,* and *Echo and Narcissus,* were as many triumphs. His life in Paris was one round of ovation and glory. The court distinguished him above all others, his relations to the Queen were those of a fatherly friend, the leaders of society coveted his friendship, and money and honours were showered on him to the gratification of his somewhat ceremonious tastes.

At an early age he had married one of his pupils, Marianne Pergin, with whom he lived in happy though childless wedlock. His adopted niece, Anna Maria Gluck, alike renowned for beauty and accomplishment, and a worthy exponent of his arias, filled the place of a daughter in his home and heart. A halo of peace and comfort was shed around the ageing man's life by these two devoted women, who appreciated at its full worth his kindly nature, which could not be obscured by occasional fits of temper.

When, therefore, his niece died in the flower of her youth, the old man, then sixty-five years of age, received a blow from which he never recovered. Two strokes of paralysis, though slight in themselves, were forebodings of death; but though the last years of his life passed in Vienna only gave birth to one opera, which bears the signs of his decadence, he struggled on bravely to the last.

It came with great suddenness. On the 15th November 1787 during a drive he became unconscious and expired the same evening in the arms of his disconsolate widow.

The same vault in the Matzlein cemetery in Vienna holds his remains and those of the two women he loved best.

But though the master is no more, his work will ever be among us. With the clairvoyance of a prophet he hailed the nascent genius of Mozart, and during his declining years pointed to him as a worthy successor to the task he had inaugurated.

A touching anecdote is related as having occurred three days before his death. It bears striking testimony to the pious simplicity which was a cornerstone to the man's character, and which finds a fitting reflection in the massive grandeur of his harmonies.

He was much impressed by the poetry of Klopstock, and it had been an unfulfilled desire to set some of his odes to music. But he felt doubts as to his ability to attune the grand words laid into the mouth of Jesus. In the course of an argument on this subject with his friend Salieri, he said, with a painful smile—

'Though I may feel doubtful now, I shall only be so for a very short time. Soon I shall be in the presence of my Saviour.'

With a merciful hand Providence removed him before the untimely fate of his revered Queen could strike horror to his heart, by the realisation of a strange spirit of prophecy which impelled him to exclaim in tones of consternation, 'Mon Dieu! there is blood on your Majesty's throat!' when he approached her one evening at a Court Concert. The fancied drops of blood were the pendent jewels of a ruby necklace encircling the fair throat.

HANDEL

1685-1759

HOWEVER startling and radical the changes that may be in store for the noble art of music in centuries to come, the great man who forms the subject of this disquisition will ever stand out as a beacon of excellence equalled by few, surpassed by none, among the long roll-call of musical heroes.

German by birth and education, a long sojourn in England endeared him to that nation, in whose Walhalla he has found a fitting resting-place among the remains of many of her noblest sons. Honour to the people which has honoured itself by the generous appreciation of genius brought forth by an alien though kindred race.

Grandeur and majesty, the principal attributes of his matchless works, loom imposingly from the mighty head and features, the massive brow, the bold outline of nose and chin, overtowered by ambrosial wig, and find their climax in the clear and fearless eye, which,

terrible in the frequent paroxysm of rage, shone
in mild benevolence when not aroused. Poor
eyes, whose lustre was haplessly fated to become obscured and shrouded in the awful night
of blindness !

With a figure tall and impressive, of herculean
framework, his every feature betokened strength,
and was in perfect keeping with the gigantic
creations of a brain of unparalleled fertility.
Sturdy in limb and sturdy in temper, we can
well imagine him fighting his bitter, desperate,
cruel fight against hopeless odds, he, single-
handed giant, against an army of pygmies. And
when at last defeat overtook him, as it was
bound to do, when energy and genius could no
longer prevail against numbers and purse power,
who but this Titan could have soared eagle-
like to heights before which the ordinary mind
stands aghast in spellbound admiration ? Who
but this Hercules could have turned into a
blessing that defeat which would have paralysed
the genius of a lesser man ?

'Obstinate to a fault' has been the verdict of
the host of his biographers, and such he had
need to be, for if Handel has become a shining
light in the world of music, this is certainly
not due to the fostering encouragement of his
early surroundings. The father, a worthy but

uncompromising surgeon, no sooner discovered the passionate fondness of the boy for his future art, than a severe interdict was laid upon all instruments that might encourage so blameable a propensity. His boy was to become a lawyer, and the sooner other fancies were discarded the better. But the five-year-old stripling had a will of his own. An old spinet was furtively introduced into the house and secreted in an attic, and while the whole household was lying in slumber, the boy would steal upstairs and indulge in such performance as his untutored fingers would command.

A few years later, accompanying his father to the Court of the Duke of Saxe-Weissenfels, the saloons and churches rang with his improvisations, until the Duke, who had been a silent witness, upbraided the father for his indifference to the boy's genius ; and, notwithstanding the counter-current of paternal obstinacy, ducal interest, even if expressed in the form of remonstrance, was not a thing to be taken lightly. Old Handel, though with a bad grace, consented to the boy receiving instruction from Zachau, and for three years a motett was the weekly contribution of the young composer to the church service.

Frederick, Elector of Brandenburg, afterwards

first King of Prussia, thought so highly of the boy's promise that he offered to send him to Italy at his expense, but for some reason the father refused this offer, and it was not until 1697, when the old man died, that his son became possessed of his freedom.

But after this event he seems to have displayed great activity in travelling and gathering information. Thus we hear of him at Leipzig, and afterwards at Hamburg, where his first opera *Almira* was performed 8th January 1705, followed closely by the second, *Nero*, on 25th February of the same year. While in that city he treated the world to a remarkable specimen of his hot temper. A quarrel with his friend Mattheson led to both young men drawing their swords, and a friendly button is said to have saved Handel from a dangerous thrust. With characteristic impulsiveness the friendship was immediately resumed, and continued without further interruption.

Shortly afterwards we find Handel at Lübeck competing for the successorship to Buxtehude, but, though otherwise eligible, he objected to a salient condition, which amounted to nothing less than that he should marry his predecessor's daughter. His refusal proved fatal, and he had to return to Hamburg. But even thus early

the fame of the composer was widespread, and
a journey through Italy in 1708 and 1709 was
a series of triumphs.   In Venice his opera
Agrippina had the unprecedented run of
twenty-seven nights, and similar successes were
achieved wherever his steps led him.

It was therefore not astonishing that the
Elector of Hanover offered most munificent
terms to secure his services.   Not only was he
allowed an ample salary, but leave was accorded
him to visit London while receiving full pay in
Hanover during his absence.   In December
1710 he first set foot in London, which city was
to become his residence, and with lightning
rapidity he wrote his first opera for the Haymarket Theatre.   The phenomenal success of
the publisher, who netted fifteen hundred pounds
out of the sale of the score, gave occasion to
one of the few jokes for which Handel was responsible.   'I propose now that the next opera
should be written by you and sold by me,' he
is reported to have said to the fortunate publisher.   Queen Anne who received him with
great distinction was most pressing that he
should return to London, and his second visit,
reluctantly permitted by his employer, took
place in 1712.   Several operas can be traced
to that visit, which also gave birth to an elabo-

rate *Te Deum* in commemoration of the Peace of Utrecht.

But the celebration of this peace gave umbrage to the Elector of Hanover, who soon afterwards ascended the throne of England as George I., and the composer, who had also offended by overstepping his leave, fell into disgrace. Several attempts at reconciliation failed, but the King could not resist the touching appeal conveyed by the celebrated *Water Music*, performed during a feast on the Thames, and his old servant was fully reinstalled in his favour.

For a number of years Handel prospered under the patronage of the Court and some of the highest of the land. Among the latter, the Earl of Burlington and the Duke of Chandos became his direct employers. Untrammelled by the cares of everyday life, operas and cantatas followed one another in unbroken succession until the foundation of the Royal Academy of Music by an influential syndicate headed by the King formed a new epoch in his career. To him was relegated the task to engage the singers, and the rival claims and endless pretensions of this self-sufficient class, seconded by partisans and aggravated by rival organisations, involved the passionate man with

endless quarrels and rendered his life nearly
intolerable.

The nobility took sides against him, and
started a rival opera which soon became a hot-
bed of intrigue, and absorbed many of those
elements whose claims Handel had rebutted.
The tenor Senesino was the most important of
his enemies. For a long time he held the
boards at Lincoln's Inn Fields Theatre, zeal-
ously supported by numerous ill-wishers of
Handel, who grouped themselves around the
composer Bononcini. Similar to the Gluck-
Piccini controversy in Paris, London was
divided into partisans of Handel and Bononcini, and a witty epigram is still extant char-
acterising the subjects of this squabble as
'Tweedledum and Tweedledee.' The after-
world is no longer in doubt as regards the
merits ; the only thing we marvel at is that
there should have ever been any doubt.

For years this fight was kept up with incredible acrimony. Defeated at the Haymarket,
Handel betook himself to the Lincoln's Inn
Fields Theatre, and spent health, money, and
energy in the vain attempt to cope with the
financial means arrayed against him. Even
his reputation suffered in this unequal combat ;
some of his later operas bear unmistakeable

traces of hasty workmanship, and none of them compare for artistic finish and freshness with those composed before 1729. Seriously compromised in health and pocket and temporarily disabled by a paralytic stroke, the master leaves the field in possession of the enemy and sets out for Tunbridge and Aix-la-Chapelle. And though he regained his health completely, the resumption of opera at the Covent Garden Theatre convinced him that in that branch of his art he had outlived his popularity.

The sufferings of his proud nature must have been intense. For a short time he was stunned, but activity was to Handel what breath is to an ordinary man. He finally, after due deliberation, fixed upon oratorio as his future field. He was not inexperienced in this branch of music. Though not so striking as his later compositions, there are extant early works of that kind which betray rare merit. Though nearly forgotten, his skill as an organist was yet undisputed. Only one possible rival existed in Bach. Everything impelled him towards oratorio; neither expense nor risk could be compared to that of opera, and, when we listen to those mighty strains which the loftiest halls and the proudest domes cannot dwarf, we only wonder that he did not discover long

before the only true outlet for his massive
genius.   For, though his opera overtopped
contemporaneous work, what remains of the
volumes over volumes written indefatigably
under the lash of hatred to a body of enemies
who ought to have been beneath the master's
notice?   Not that his operatic works are without gems of a high order, but can they bear
comparison with the majestic strains of the
Messiah, Samson, Judas Maccabæus, and many
others which bid fair to survive the obliterating
waves of Time as the Egyptian pyramids have
triumphantly withstood the gnawing tooth of
centuries?

This last crowning era of the master's fame
is also an astounding proof of his vitality.   It
has been said that genius is definable as
capacity for hard work.   If this be the case
we know of no worthier claimant of the title
of genius.   Fifty-seven years old, bowed down
by bitter disappointment, his frame racked by
disease, the master not only strikes out a new
path but compasses his own apotheosis at a
time when most mortals sigh for rest and willingly relinquish their field of action to younger
generations.   How shall we qualify that brain
which in twenty-four days gave birth to the
monumental harmonies of the *Messiah,* whose

every number teems with soul-stirring ideas, threaded together in so masterly a manner, in so ingenious a structure, that even the skill of a Mozart, while adding some instruments, despaired of increasing its solid grandeur?

For eight years he delighted the world with his matchless creations. Thirteen oratorios flowed from his pen and challenged the echo of unbounded enthusiasm. Never had the fame of the composer stood so high; never had applause been showered on him with a more ungrudging hand. The indignation of a whole people was aroused when an envious coterie attempted to forbid his performances under some sophisticated plea. Abashed, the detractors withdrew, while the object of their enmity became an idol of popular worship.

But a blow, the hardest of all, was at hand. In 1750 his eyesight declined, and in 1751 total blindness supervened. *Jephthah* was his last work; it is written in a handwriting vastly changed, and unspeakably touching is the quotation written at foot in trembling letters :—

, ' Sweet as sight to the blind.'

Twice he was operated on for cataract, but when he found that his doom was sealed, he submitted with that courage which was in keeping with his manly character. For eight years he lingered, calmly quiet. A marked decline overtook him in 1758, but his robust constitution enabled him to struggle on till 1759, when he expired on Good Friday, 13th April, his last wish being that his life should terminate on that auspicious day. Had he been a prince or a victorious general his obsequies could not have been attended with greater splendour. The venerable Abbey seemed hushed in awe. The Bishop of Rochester officiated to the strains of the composer's own funeral anthem. A whole people mourned the decease of this man who blended simplicity with majesty, and whose courage in days of woe was equalled by his unassuming modesty in the zenith of his glory.

Great stress has been laid on his violence of temper, and, unless all accounts are untrue, we cannot exonerate the master from this blame. The man who held a recalcitrant prima donna out of the window until she consented to sing, who struck the violin from the hands of Corelli for a difference of opinion, and whom the presence of the Court would not prevent from swearing at ladies who did not preserve strict silence during his performances, cannot by any stretch of imagination be adjudged an angel of meekness. The reproach must stand, though it may be added in extenuation that, if his wrath was terrible, it was also shortlived. This and the charge of intemperance in eating are the only exceptions taken to his character. It is difficult to refute them when practically nothing is known of the accused's private life, and that, for this very good reason, that he had, properly speaking, no private life. A man of such indomitable pluck, and overwhelmed with the wealth of ideas which enabled him to write his masterpiece in a few weeks, not to mention the endless pile of other compositions stapled up in the Royal library, had no room for private life. From morning to noon and deep into the night he worked without losing a moment. Invitations, showered on him, were invariably refused; and only two or three people had admission to his house. The spinet on which he thundered forth his ideas had little rest; after his death it was found that the keys were scooped out by constant usage until they took the shape of spoons. No wife ever ministered to his comforts or soothed his joyless age; no love affair ever had possession of his mind; in a state of strict celibacy he devoted his entire existence to his art, the only exception being a remarkable love of the sister art of painting, evidenced by a small but valuable collection of pictures gradually acquired.   He did not shine as a man of letters or linguistic attainments ; a good knowledge of Italian was indispensable for a musician of those days, and his English though necessarily comprehensive was marred by a very strong German accent.

It has often been attempted to draw a parallel between Handel and his great contemporary Bach, but beyond a great proficiency in manipulating the organ, common to both, there are many points of divergence.   While Bach will ever remain caviare to the masses and accessible only to the select few, Handel was an essentially popular composer, in constant touch with the people, and, though far from pandering to their taste, intrinsically an exponent of music that found its way to the heart of the many.   Bach, therefore, though of the greatest influence on the music of all times, has only become so through other, less profound, writers, who, adopting his ideas and teachings, have filtered them into a shape easier to understand.   Handel cannot be said to have founded a new school.   He had neither time nor inclination to surround himself with disciples who must have been his inferiors, and who would have probably not been bedded on roses.   Smith, whom he trained to conduct his oratorios, was nothing but a respectable mediocrity. His mission was to place on record the torrent of ideas which must have filled his brain to overflowing. Nor was he influenced by contemporary tendencies. Handel was Handel and nothing besides. Would the Niagara be more majestic if fed by another tributary river? Without despising his coevals he had no time to devote to their music; and while Bach eagerly sought acquaintance with those whom he thought worth cultivating, Handel had no such inclination. A depreciating estimate of Gluck is indeed on record, but then it does not refer to Gluck's happier efforts. Bach tried repeatedly to make the acquaintance of Handel, and made two abortive journeys for that purpose. There is no mention of any eagerness on the part of Handel to meet the man who was widely considered his equal.

But though comparisons between great men will be ever attractive, it is more than difficult to arrive at conclusive opinions. The world has reason to be thankful that Bach and Handel have existed to enrich its knowledge. Both were great among the great; both of strongly pronounced individuality carried to a high degree of perfection. Why indulge in futile speculations as to which was the greater?

HAYDN

1732-1809

IF Bach is justly esteemed the originator of
the new style of music which in the latter
part of the eighteenth century revolutionised
the Italian school, Haydn has the undisputed
claim to being the first to apply these principles
to instrumental music, and thus not only
establish his own undying fame, but smooth
the way for his eminent contemporaries and
successors, Mozart and Beethoven.

Though the former may be his superior in
passion and intensity, and the latter in energy,
grandeur, and solemnity, there is a quiet, childlike simplicity, the ineffable charm of innocence
and gay good humour, in Haydn's compositions
which has never been equalled in the history of
music, and from which the new style of music
is drifting apart with great steps. But, however
great the changes that have been wrought in
style and conception since he has disappeared
from the stage, succeeding generations have

112

stood in wondering admiration before his chaste
and sunny tone poems, revealing in their every
tone the purity of soul and guileless temperament of their conceiver.

It is believed that the family of Haydn, or
Haiden as the name was originally spelt, can
be traced back to Bohemia, but it can only be
said with certainty that the father, Matthias
Haydn, lived at Rohrau, a small town near the
Hungarian frontier, where Joseph was born on
the 31st March 1732, not on the 1st of April,
as has been erroneously stated by some biographers. He was the eldest of a family of
nine, of which two younger boys embraced the
musical career with moderate success. His
parentage was of the simplest : the father
united the functions of wagoner, justice of the
peace, beadle and organist ; and the mother
had been cook to Count Harrach, the local
magnate. But—what is more to the point—
they were both gifted with some vocal and
instrumental talents, and not beyond regaling
their fellow villagers with music on Sundays
and holidays, the wife accompanying her husband on the harp.

At an early age young Joseph evinced signs
of musical talent, and, while his parents plied
their voice and instruments, he would sit on a

H

low stool with two sticks, pretending to use them as a violin.   Unimportant though this appears, it must have had no small influence on the boy's career.   An uncle at Hainburg, struck by the evident sense of rhythm and time displayed by the boy in his make-belief pro- fession, offered to charge himself with his education, and the parents, none too well off, accepted gladly.

For three years Hainburg was his home, and though a little better treatment and a more liberal fare might have been acceptable, these three years were of considerable use to him, on his own admission, as having been the means of storing his mind with a fundamental knowledge of music, reading, writing, Latin, and elementary violin playing.   He was eight years old when by accident, Reuter, leader of the St. Stephen's choir at Vienna, arrived at Hainburg in search of choristers.   He consented to hear young Haydn, and gave him a task, of which the boy acquitted himself creditably, with the exception of the trills, with which the master found fault.

'How should I be able to trill,' young Joseph said, 'when my master himself cannot do it?'

'Come here, then,' said the visitor, and he was quite charmed to find that his pupil

followed his instructions with the greatest
facility.

Thus Haydn entered the choir of St.
Stephen's and laid the beginning of his grand
career. His duties were not onerous, but all
his spare time was taken up by ceaseless efforts
to obtain mastery of everything pertaining to
music. To hear a performance of any kind
was his principal delight ; the intonation of the
organ in the venerable cathedral was for him
the signal to quit his games in spite of the
taunts of his playfellows. When about thirteen
he felt impelled to compose, and started on
some trifles, but soon trifles sufficed for him
no longer. He wrote a mass, and showed the
score to Reuter, who, however, laughed at him,
saying that he ought first to learn to write.
The boy, much chagrined, felt nevertheless the
justice of this remark, and determined to
launch into the necessary studies at once.
Unfortunately, he knew of no master who
would teach him without pay, and this he was
unable to afford. In his despair he wrote to
his father asking for some money for repairs to
clothes. The good man sent him six florins,
which were forthwith invested in the *Gradus
ad Parnassum*, by Fox, and the *Parfait Maître
de Chapelle*, by Mattheson, and now commenced

a course of assiduous and unrelenting study. But though these works were devoured with insatiable appetite, he did not accord an unqualified agreement to all the principles therein contained, and showed thus early that he felt the vocation to strike out a course for himself.

Over eight years Haydn remained at St. Stephen's, well known for his excellent voice, and in high favour with the director, Reuter ; indeed, so favourably was this latter impressed with the boy's talents, that he offered to take his two younger brothers, Michael and Johann, into the choir, and promised the father to secure their future, an offer which must have gladdened the hearts of the brave but needy old people. But, approaching the age of puberty, Joseph's voice grew weaker, and at last his connection with the cathedral was severed rather abruptly. The year in which this took place has been variously stated between 1747 and 1750, the latter period being perhaps more probable. There is also considerable doubt as to the immediate cause which led to Haydn's dismissal from the choir in something like disgrace. Some authorities allege professional jealousy on the part of Reuter, others mention a puerile escapade, in the course of which one of his colleagues would seem to have been deprived of his pig-tail. But it seems certain that the parting was not friendly, and that for one night poor Haydn had to camp in the street without a roof to his head. On the next day a temporary make-shift was offered to him by a friend or acquaintance, himself in needy circumstances, which was gratefully accepted. Again doubts prevail as to the person of this benefactor. A suggestion has been thrown out that it was a certain Spangler, but this cannot be reconciled with chronological circumstances, and the theory that it was the barber Keller, destined afterwards to become the composer's father-in-law, though interesting from that reason, cannot be satisfactorily substantiated.

A journey to Mariazell, and an unsuccessful application to join the choir, which the young enthusiast circumvented by taking the law in his own hand, would also appear to have fallen in this period, which is altogether veiled in great obscurity ; but anyhow, Haydn emerges from it after a time as an eager student of music, afflicted with great poverty, but still enabled to devote himself to his favourite study, and even boasting the coveted possession of a piano of questionable excellence.

His parents, much disappointed at his refusal to enter the church, seemed to have made up their mind to the inevitable.   A wonderful impetus was given to his creative genius by the first six sonatas of Emanuel Bach, and he often confessed to a debt of sincere gratitude towards this master.   Occasional engagements with orchestras and poorly-paid tuition of piano were his only sources of income, until an unexpected stroke of fortune procured him the acquaintance of the poet Metastasio, and through him of the singing-master Porpora, who engaged him as accompanist, and although his position was still far from brilliant, as may be imagined from the fact that he had to board with the servants, his emoluments increased steadily from that time to his death, and of actual misery, such as shortened the days of Mozart and many others, Haydn had only a very short spell.

Many of his smaller sonatas, trios, and serenades date from this time, also his acquaintance with the actor Bernardone, at whose instance he wrote an opera, *The Crooked Devil*, which was suppressed after a few performances owing to personalities which occasioned complaint.   The Countess Thun also proved a valuable acquaintance for him, and she it was, probably, who procured him a situation with Count Haugwitz, and another at a cathedral in the Leopoldstadt.

Altogether Haydn seems to have had great aptitude in inspiring others with sympathy, and when a burglary deprived him of all his possessions, the loss was made good immediately by friends, and temporary quarters found for him in the house of a Baron Fürnberg, who was a great enthusiast for music, and gave regular concerts at his place near Vienna. It was here Haydn made the acquaintance of the well-known composer Albrechtsberger. But if most of his connections proved of great advantage, this was not the case with the barber, Keller, to whose daughters he gave lessons. Various opinions exist as to the commencement of this friendship, which was destined to have such unfortunate results. Certain it is that after some time Haydn took up his abode with the family altogether. Keller himself seems to have behaved with great generosity, laying his guest under undoubted obligations. A tender attachment towards the elder daughter, which was fully reciprocated, promised well, but her death supervened and led to the one fatal step, which cast a blight over the days of the composer, binding him to the younger daughter, whom he thought himself in duty bound to marry.

His residence with the Keller family lasted till 1758 or 1759, when he was offered a good engagement with Count Morzin, a Bohemian nobleman. Here he made the acquaintance of Prince Paul Esterhazy, who greatly admired one of his symphonies, and wished at that time to engage him. Soon afterwards Count Morzin was compelled by pecuniary reasons to dismiss his orchestra, and on the 1st May 1761 Haydn entered the service of Prince Esterhazy. 'Blacka- moor,' the nobleman is reported to have said to the swarthy composer, 'you are henceforth in my service.' But for all that he proved a kind master, and with him and his successors Haydn was to pass many years to come. The written agreement has been recently unearthed ; it is a most ponderous document, enumerating a host of duties that were to come within the range of his office, and laying special stress on the proper attention to pigtail, powder, and dress, and the practice of sobriety. The salary commencing with 400 florins was gradually raised until it stood at 1000 florins, a formidable amount for those times.

From this period onwards Haydn's pecuniary position was always assured, and his fame, already considerable, grew as the years, and with them the number of his works, increased. Symphonies, quartets, trios, sonatas, took shape in never-ending array under the prolific pen of the master, whose favour with his employers was ever increasing. Noire, his house, in the little town of Gisenstadt, was burnt to the ground, and on each occasion it was built up again by his munificent patron. A number of operas were composed, among which *Acis and Galatea*, *La vera Costanga*, and *Armida*, are best known by name, but being all intended for the miniature stage at Esterház, they have scarcely been suitable to larger theatres. Of the piles of sacred music, cantatas, arias, etc., which belong to that period, in oratorio, *Il Ritorno di Tòbias* deserves mention as having led to a long estrangement with the Vienna Widows' and Orphans' Society, who, not content with the composer's permission to perform his work free of charge, mulcted him in a heavy fine which some antiquated law imposed on compositions not written at Vienna.

Haydn's fame soon spread beyond the confines of his country. In 1780 the Philharmonic Society of Modena made him an honorary member, and in 1784 six quartets, dedicated to Prince Henry of Prussia, procured him a

medal and the portrait of that Prince. A
valuable diamond ring was the present of
Frederick William II. of Prussia, for a cantata
on the death of Frederick the Great. Even to
a town as distant as Cadiz the master's name
had penetrated, as evidenced by an order that
reached him for church music.

And now an important landmark in his
career has been reached. Many attempts had
been made to induce the composer to undertake voyages to France, Italy, and England,
but attachment to his employer had always
prevented his doing so. In London his works
were well known, and formed a staple attraction
in all concert programmes. A Professional
Concert Society was formed in 1783, under
the presidentship of Lord Aberdeen, but all
endeavours to lure the celebrated composer into
their midst were of no avail.

At last a private impresario succeeded where
the Society had failed. The death of Prince
Nicholas Esterhazy and the accession of his
son, who had no taste for music, led to Haydn's
retirement with an ample pension, and this,
coinciding with repeated pressure of the London
agent, led to an agreement and eventually to
his departure for London, the composer being
laudably careful to have all payments guaranteed,

and a considerable sum of money deposited with a Vienna banker.

On the 2nd of January 1791 Haydn and Salomon arrived in London and passed the first night at No. 45 Holborn, whence they moved on the next day to No. 18 Pulteney Street. His impressions of London and the hearty welcome accorded to him on all hands seem to have been invariably favourable. A series of twelve concerts was advertised, and, after several postponements, the first one actually took place on March 11th. The delay was vexatious, as it enabled the Professional Society to forestall him ; but their programme, which contained many of his compositions, was a further tribute to his name, and every one of his twelve appearances was a brilliant success, his benefit concert, which took place on May 16th, netting £350.

The stay in London lasted about eighteen months. During the whole of this time the composer was made the subject of unqualified applause and admiration. For the first time he was enabled to drink in Handel's music in its full glory, and the effect appears to have been imposing in the extreme. Among other pageants he makes frequent reference to the conferring of the Oxford degree of Mus. D., and the Lord Mayor's dinner in the following year, besides many receptions by the Prince of Wales and one by the King, who treated him with the greatest distinction. Professional jealousies created an occasional sound of discord, but not of a lasting nature.

At last, in July 1792, he left England for Vienna, making a halt at Bonn. Here he met young Beethoven for the first time, and expressed himself favourably of a cantata composed by the latter. Most probably it was arranged on this occasion that he should instruct the young man. Much has been written about the estrangement between the two which led to an early separation. The older master has been openly accused of motives of jealousy, but this is hardly likely. In the first place, we can scarcely believe that the feeling of jealousy found room in Haydn's genial temper, and though later on Beethoven overshadowed his whilom teacher, this was not the case at the early stage when the elder man was in the zenith of his fame. But two men more unlike each other could scarcely be imagined, and a lasting attachment between the sunny and childlike geniality of the one and the dark and tempestuous soul of the other seems nearly impossible.

After an uneventful winter in Vienna Haydn set out on his second visit to London, where he arrived February 4th, 1794. He had scarcely landed when news came of the death of Prince Paul Esterhazy and the desire of his successor to re-establish the orchestra under Haydn's leadership. Highly pleased, he at once intimated his willingness to resume his old position as soon as his engagements would permit him to leave England. The 15th August was the last day spent in that country, which besides honour and glory had enriched him by over two thousand pounds.

The next years of his life were passed in full enjoyment of health and honour. His pecuniary position was brilliant compared with that of most of his contemporaries, and, with the one exception of his unhappy marriage, there was no cloud on the horizon to dim his happiness and rob his music of that simple joyfulness which is its characteristic. The two oratorios, *The Creation* and *The Seasons*, composed at that time, and the soul-stirring national hymn, *God save Franz the Emperor*, a pathetic reply to the levelling influence of the French revolution, are among his noblest works ; but an enumeration of the endless number of trios, quartets, solos, symphonies, etc. etc., would far exceed the limits of this work.

After 1802 his nerves became much shattered, and the death of his two brothers in 1805 and 1806 was a hard blow to the old man. One last appropriate triumph was in store for him on March 27th, 1808, when on the occasion of a performance of the *Creation* the aged master was acclaimed with trumpets and cymbals. After that he sank rapidly. On May 31st, 1809, the roar of the French cannon, plainly discernible from the master's house, formed a sinister accompaniment to his death struggle. Muttering the words of his national hymn, *Gott erhalte Franz den Kaiser*, the old man fell back in his chair and ended a long and honourable life.

His wife had preceded him in 1800, after having lived separated from him for a number of years.

The music of Haydn will ever be remarkable for a charm of simplicity essentially its own. Of the triumvirate whose fame bids fair to outlast centuries his lot alone was cast in happy lines, and there is absent from his music alike the plaintive wail which in piteous vibration traverses the effusions of unhappy Mozart, and the solemn grandeur of the titanic thunderbolts which flashed from beneath the shaggy brow of Beethoven.

His was a bucolic, patriarchal mind, suited to the time of his youth and manhood, and out of touch with the stormy events which overshadowed his declining days.

MENDELSSOHN

1809-1847

LIKE a wounded boar, Germany was smarting under the ruthless heel of Napoleon's ambition. The Austrians, sorely tried, rose up in arms for a second time, but the battle of Wagram put an end to their hopes, and the roar of the French cannon outside Vienna, besides destroying many fervid aspirations, was not without musical significance, as it sounded the death knell of old Father Haydn. With a tremulous hand and a voice enfeebled by age and emotion, he had sounded his own glorious hymn, *Gott erhalte Franz den Kaiser,* as a silent but ineffectual protest against the giant upheaval, which, among so much of antiquated glory, had shattered the German Imperial crown. And who could have forseen that in distant Berlin, saddened by early bereavement, humiliated by a relentless despot, the shadow of that proud fabric reared up by the genius of Frederick—that stripling of twelve, marching by the side of his father's

128

giant grenadiers, a second son, should grow up into that regenerator of the defunct empire, whom, only a few years ago, we have seen carried to an honoured grave, bowed down by years, and victories, and honours—the arbiter of Europe?

A troublous year, forsooth, that year of 1809, which gave birth to the composer who forms the subject of these remarks!

Hamburg, the birth-place of Mendelssohn, under the yoke of Davoust, was the scène of cruelties which have made that name a by-word of iniquity. Life in the ancient Hanse town became so intolerable that the parents, though encumbered with three little children, resolved to transfer their residence to Berlin, and in this city, his favourite aversion of later years, the boy passed a happy childhood and youth, in the security and charm of the most affectionate family ties.

The name of Mendelssohn was not without its heritage of fame. In 1786, Moses Mendelssohn, the grandfather of Felix, had died at Berlin, greatly honoured by the best among his contemporaries as the foremost Jewish philosopher since Spinoza. Abraham, his second son, coming between an illustrious father and an equally famous son, used to say of

I

himself, that in his youth he had been known as the son of his father, and later on as the father of his son. But, though overshadowed by the superior genius of his nearest of kin, he seems on all accounts to have been a man of great merit and rare common-sense, and from every point of view well qualified to foster the talent which was under his care.

Eminently artistic, both father and mother stood out among art-loving families of the residence ; talent of any kind was a free passport to their hospitable house, and yet it is difficult to decide whence the musical gifts of all their children have been derived. It is characteristic that, in spite of the early promise of the boy, the father doubted for a long time that music was his real vocation. This did not, however, prevent the greatest attention being given to the musical development of the boy and his eldest sister, Fanny, who was possessed of considerable talent. Berger and Zelter were engaged as tutors, and the precocious genius of their charge was so phenomenal as to recall the early days of Mozart. Zelter, most fastidious of teachers, waxes enthusiastic in his letters to Goethe about this young pupil. On February 2, 1824, when the boy was scarcely fifteen, we find an allusion in one of the letters to his '*fourth* opera,' and a little later, on 22nd December of the same year, to a '*new* double concert,' while a psalm is mentioned much before that, in 1821, as having been received with great applause.

His earliest compositions lean towards the strictly classical style, but a decided departure was to take place when he became acquainted with the compositions of Weber. The style affected by that composer exercised a potent spell over the young enthusiast, and the Overture to the *Midsummer Night's Dream* amounts to a sudden complete conversion to the 'romantic' school.

The memorable movement which under that name took possession of all German thought originated, no doubt, in a widespread sympathy with the course of political events. The fervid enthusiasm which had nerved the whole people into that irresistible uprising against which the genius of Napoleon could no longer prevail had been painfully damped by the narrow-minded maxims of Metternich and his satellites, anxious only to keep out every breath of individuality, to repress every atom of that sacred inheritance bequeathed by the best traditions of the French Revolution. In despair, the Ro-

mancers turned' away from the poverty of contemporary surroundings and dived into the
traditions of the Dark Ages and the uncertain
mirage of Indian and Persian folklore, extolling
into fancied brilliancy, and with a total disregard of actuality, any age rather than their
own.

For a long time this tendency reigned supreme
in poetry. Werther-like, without the realistic
power of that sublime impersonation, the productions of their pen were remarkable for a
morbid unreality and a want of depth for which
no beauty of language or mastery of form could
atone.

In music this school was not without its adherents. Schubert and Schumann, though not
without an admixture of the spirit of their age,
may be considered its more vigorous exponents,
and it is difficult to reconcile the manly force
of the latter with his devoted admiration of the
literature of Jean Paul. But a more pronounced
master of the purely romantic style arose in
Weber, whose *libretti*, deeply dipped into mystic
fancy and dark superstition, are ably interpreted by his music; and among all Weber's
followers, none interpreted his peculiarities
with greater effect than Mendelssohn. Though
not without its beauties, the romantic style of

music has been reproached for a conspicuous want of depth, and the greatest admirer of Mendelssohn cannot gainsay the fact that the broad, monumental style of Bach and Beethoven, and the sweet intensity of Mozart, are not to be found in his works. The elegant sylph-like movement which, like a silvery brook, pervades the score of the *Midsummer Night's Dream*, the ineffable longing in some of his songs, notably *I Would that my Love* and *On love's bright pinions*, appeal to us as graceful wishes for an unknown something, beautiful plaints sighing for the impenetrable, fanciful, unrealistic, indefinable even by the author, negative as compared with the eloquent vigour of the old masters, whose language takes a definite shape accessible only to its admirers.

Something of this kind may have occurred to the practical mind of the father, and impelled him to seek the advice of unquestionable authorities before allowing his son to launch into music as a vocation. With this object he made a journey to Paris, and sought the opinion of Cherubini. The verdict was most flattering, and had the more value considering the well-known brusqueness of the old Italian, who was, as a rule, very sparing of compliments, and prone to indulge in satirical sneers when confronted with mediocrity. But with Felix he was so well pleased that he offered to charge himself with his training, and, though the offer was not accepted, the vocation of the young man was now admitted without further hesitation.

The return journey is remarkable for a visit to Goethe, whose correspondence bears ample trace of the esteem in which he held the young composer. The musical studies are now resumed with the greatest vigour, but do not prevent a regular attendance at the University and ample researches in philosophy and history. A number of public performances fell within that period, but the best opportunities to hear Felix were afforded by the private concerts held regularly at his parents' house, and eagerly attended by all that was most prominent in the walks of art. Four operas were thus rehearsed and played before a private audience, but, as they have never been submitted to a public test, we may assume that their intrinsic merit may not have been great.

The fifth opera, *The Wedding of Camacho*, was produced on the Berlin stage after considerable opposition, but the reception was not favourable. To this circumstance, and to the candour of some critics, may be attributed the marked aversion towards Berlin as a musical resort, which rankled in the breast of Mendelssohn until his death, and which the most brilliant subsequent successes could never quite obliterate. It did not, however, prevent his active connection with the Singakademie, into which he carefully instilled an appreciation of the old masters, foreign to that age of musical decrepitude. If Mendelssohn had no merits of his own as composer and musician, his name would deserve mention for the service he rendered by exhuming so many gems of the first value, and thus generally rehabilitating the classical masters in the place which is their just due. The grand *Matthaeus Passion* by Bach, which did so much to stimulate the universal study of this sublime composer, might still be unknown but for the unremitting activity of Mendelssohn. Berlin, prejudiced though it was, became fairly electrified by the mighty harmonies of this mass, and a second performance was vociferously demanded.

But a greater reception awaited the master in England, where Moscheles had with commendable disinterestedness paved the way for his successful rival. His title to a foremost place among pianists, orchestra-leaders, and composers was acclaimed with an enthusiasm

unknown since Handel and Haydn had wielded
the baton.   The Overture to the *Midsummer
Night's Dream* evoked   an   applause   which
drowned the previous successes of Weber, whose
visit was still fresh in the memory of the English.
Mendelssohn never forgot his debt of gratitude
to his insular friends.   Coming so close upon
the real or fancied wrongs experienced in Berlin,
the demonstration gained by contrast.   Nor
are the Londoners without obligations towards
their celebrated guest, for indeed the man,
eminent or not, who can call London, on
November 6th, 'indescribably beautiful,' and
write from Italy that he longs to be back in
'dear, smoky London,' deserves a wreath at
the hands of the gloomy, if colossal, metropolis.
But though from a musical point of view the
English gave Mendelssohn occasion for many
a hearty laugh, he was in thorough touch with
his audience, and he could appreciate the applause which nowhere else had been meted out
to him with so ungrudging a hand.   And, indeed,
many reminiscences go to prove that he was
the spoilt child of all circles, from the Royal
household at Windsor down to the most insignificant member of his orchestra.   Only one
exception has to be placed on record, and that
is to his honour as an impartial and just—

perhaps too just—appreciation of the music of his contemporaries. He had arranged to produce the Symphony in C by Schubert, a Symphony in C minor by Gade, and his own Overture to *Ruy Blas*; but the first two pieces were somewhat coldly received by the band, and this so exasperated the impressionable enthusiast that with rare abnegation he refused to have his own work performed; it remained unheard in England until after his death.

Returning from the first visit to England, he undertakes his voyage to Italy. At Weimar he makes his first halt. The great poet, who from this place still diffused his lustre over Germany and the world, holds him in charmed spell. From day to day the departure is postponed, until a projected stay of a day has been magnified into a fortnight. It was his last meeting with the majestic Olympian, the last God-speed he was to receive from those revered lips. At Munich he takes another rest; there, as everywhere, he enchants his audience and reaps a phenomenal success with his overture, *Return from Abroad*, composed in celebration of the silver wedding of his parents. But wherever he goes his principal aim is to re-establish the worship of the old masters, temporarily obscured by the trivial melodies of

Kalkbrenner, Hünten, Ascher, and their worthless display of shallow fireworks based on operatic banalities.

From Italy he writes in expressions of rapture about the beauties of nature and art, at the shrine of which all lovers of art should bow in admiration ; but the Italian music disgusts him, and receives unqualified condemnation at his hands. A chance meeting with Madame von Ertmann, the friend of Beethoven, and with a son of Mozart, ' who, though official, is,' as he writes, ' a musician at heart,' rekindles all his love and admiration for these masters, whose worship is ever uppermost in his mind, untroubled by the rival claims of romanticism. But Italian impressions may be best gathered from the published volume of letters, specimens of rare literary excellence in themselves. Among them is one to his adored sister Fanny, containing the first of his *Songs without Words*. He characterises it as an expression of what he would wish to convey to her by word of mouth, but is compelled by distance to express in music.

After an agreeable stay in Rome he shapes his course towards Paris, where, however, he was only moderately appreciated. The stay in this town, aggravated by an attack of cholera, cannot have been pleasant, especially as the

death of his friend Rietz was the first of the
series of blows which did so much to cut short
his own career in its prime.   A few days later
the death of Goethe cast a pall over Europe,
and must have been severely felt by his young
friend.

London came as a relief after these *contre-
temps*.   The *Hebrides* overture was performed
to an audience turbulent in its demonstrations
of delight.   And still death was busy.   Zelter's
was the next to darken his brow, and an ill-
advised and worse-managed competition for
his successorship at the Berlin Singakademie,
which met with defeat, cast a shadow over the
ambitious mind of Mendelssohn, and intensified
the estrangement he felt for Berlin.

But the *Reformation Symphony* and the
Walpurgisnacht music soon occupied all his
attention, and a call to Düsseldorf claimed
much of his time and curtailed his productive-
ness during that period.   Though not unsuccessful in his attempt to raise the musical
standard of the Rhenish town, he eclipsed his
own efforts at Leipzig, which town he raised to
the first place in Germany, and indeed in the
world, as arbiter of music.   For excellence of
taste, skill of execution, and truly classical
tendency the *Gewandhaus* concerts were un-

rivalled, and maintained their reputation for years after the founder had ceased to be among the living.   To be considered of the first rank, every musician had to make his bow to the Leipzig audience and submit to the leaders of the Conservatory assembled in conclave, an areopagus, severely just, and unpitying to mediocrity, but frankly appreciative of real genius, and unswayed by petty considerations of jealousy.

The composer was at work on his oratorio *St. Paul* when the hardest blow he had yet experienced overtook him.   On the 19th November 1835 his father died suddenly, without having embraced his beloved son.   The grief of Mendelssohn was unspeakable ; for a long time he was not the same man.   Indeed, it may be well doubted whether the loss of that father, who to him had been guardian, friend, and companion, was ever completely overcome. Had it not been for the oratorio, which he pushed forward in compliance with the last request of the departed, the consequences might have even been more severe ; but hard work, though it could not obliterate his grief, went a long way towards soothing his spirit into the welcome oblivion of fatigue induced by close study and mental concentration.

In 1837, during a visit to Frankfort, he met the woman who was to sweeten the last years of his existence. Cécile Jeanrenaud, the daughter of a French Protestant clergyman, was endowed with all the graces of a beautiful presence and a sympathetic soul. Her virtues are enshrined in the touching eloquence of his letters, which one and all refer to her, and the children born of their marriage, in terms of the greatest love. Up to his death she remained his devoted companion, and when the beloved husband sank into an early grave, followed by the son, with whom he had loved to play and gambol, a veritable child himself in the innocent enjoyment of the boy's company, she only survived for a few years, unconsoled, because nothing could console her, for the losses she had experienced.

We may seem to anticipate, but in reality the declining years of Mendelssohn are already dimly foreshadowed in an increased nervousness, and the appalling effect on his highly-strung sensitive organisation of troubles, even of the most trivial nature, which caused his hair to blanch prematurely, and imparted an unmistakeable stamp of weariness to his genial countenance.

In 1846 Frederick William IV. ascended the throne of Prussia. This eminently gifted and

artistic prince, who had always appreciated
Mendelssohn at his real merits, offered him
magnificent terms for the superintendence of
an academy to be established in Berlin. The
negotiations occupied a long time, and, though
the master accepted, his dislike of Berlin, which,
from the frequency of its manifestation, would
appear to have been somewhat unjust and
founded on prejudice, precluded his ever co-
operating cordially with his confrères. A great
deal of vexation, endless letters and documents,
and abortive proposals and counter-proposals,
were a source of constant irritation ; and, though
the King was invariably considerate and indulgent towards the most unreasonable whims of
his irritable subject, the connection was always
half-hearted. A continued disregard of the
King's wishes gave rise to an ill-feeling which
was not altogether without grounds. At last
they parted, Mendelssohn retaining the title
and the somewhat irregular functions of a Royal
Prussian *Kapellmeister*, with the permission to
reside at Leipzig. The bestowal soon afterwards of the high Prussian *Ordre pour le Mérite*
was a graceful tribute on the part of the royal
Maecenas, which deserved a better reception
than the sneer it elicited from some of the
composer's contemporaries.

Voyages to Frankfort and England, and a quiet uneventful life at Leipzig, fill the last years of the master. *Elijah* follows his successful oratorio of *St. Paul*, and, though weary and melancholy, his music preserved its standard of excellence unimpaired to the last.

A vexatious incident occurred to hasten the sad event. Returning from England, he was made the subject of police inquiry directed at a different man of the same name. The nervous tension of the moribund master became well-nigh intolerable under this indignity, and when, in this frame of mind, he was suddenly informed of the death of his beloved sister, the blow fell on receptive ground.

Two slight strokes of paralysis acted like thunderbolts on his shattered nerves. For a short time he lingered, the object of the hushed sympathy of all Leipzig, and when the end came at 9 p.m. of the 14th of May, the mourning in which the whole of Germany seemed plunged was as intense as it was sincere. It was nearly equalled in England, where the people had long regarded him in somewhat the light of a successor to Handel.

Mendelssohn's influence on music outlasted his life. For a long time young composers tried as well as they could to follow in his footsteps, and the more virile music of Schumann and Brahms would possibly have received earlier recognition had it not been for the transcendental worship of their contemporary. And, though the romantic school has been superseded by the worship of Schumann, Wagner, and the older and more positive masters, the graceful elegance of Mendelssohn stands in no danger of being swept from the boards, though it may be regretted that a master so superior in all the highest works of his art has in many instances sacrificed substance to somewhat superficial melody. In saying this we quote the opinion of many eminent composers, to suspect whom of jealousy there is no reason. But whoever has heard the incomparable Overture to the *Midsummer Night's Dream, Hebrides, Ruy Blas, Melusine*, the Violin Concerto, and so many other monuments of vocal and instrumental beauty, may well ask whether a heavier instrumentation would not detract from their elfin-like charms.

It is not generally known that Mendelssohn was no mean adept at drawing, that he has left a great number of sketches of considerable artistic value, and that as a letter-writer he has not many superiors. Indeed the quantity of his letters, and the minute care devoted to every stroke of his pen and every tone of his musical manuscripts, cause the spectator to marvel at the time he must have spent over these apparent trifles. The methodical neatness in which all his papers are arranged forms the surprised delight of researchers, who are not spoilt by the somewhat slovenly tendencies generally connected with genius.

It is also a remarkable fact that Mendelssohn was a good gymnast, swimmer, and rider, a passionate dancer, and of fair skill at chess and billiards.

In appearance he was short and delicate looking, Semitic in type, with wonderful eyes, which seemed to dilate to a marvellous degree when inspired. His nature was kindly, and, sensitive himself to adverse criticism, he shrank from wounding others. Towards contemporaries he was most indulgent and frankly appreciative, even of those who, like Berlioz, were artistically opposed to him.

K

MEYERBEER

1791-1864

HOT strife has raged around the name of this composer. Musical critics of all classes and shades have freely condemned him, and friendly voices have been few and far between. Wagner himself, by no means one of the least abused composers, has emptied the vial of his wrath and sarcasm over the head of Meyerbeer, whose exertions in his behalf, when, half starving, he sought the suffrages of the Paris public, the immortal composer of *Lohengrin* deliberately ignored.

As a set-off against adverse comment, we are confronted by stubborn facts, amounting to actual successes hitherto unknown and undreamt of, success conveyed by the lusty voices of thousands, and substantiated by a flood-tide of money, such as has fallen to the lot of no operatic composer before or since. It is remarkable that these very successes form the basis of all the indictments hurled with more or less vituperative eloquence at the devoted head of a man generally esteemed as kindly and amiable.

'My heart bleeds,' writes C. M. von Weber, who nevertheless preserved for Meyerbeer an affectionate friendship and a warm appreciation of his great gifts to his death, 'to see a German composer of creative power stoop to become an imitator, in order to win favour with the crowd.' 'He is going to settle in Berlin,' occurs in a later letter, 'where, perhaps, he will write a German opera. Please God he may! I made many appeals to his conscience.' Wagner is less indulgent. While regretting the mistaken tendency of his friend, Weber never for a moment doubts his abilities; but the judgment of the latter master disdains any reservation on this score. 'A miserable music maker,' 'a Jew banker, to whom it occurred to compose operas,' are a few of the epithets scattered broadcast with a lavish hand, and a pen steeped in scathing sarcasm and the bitterest of venom. We can well imagine that a composer who was both rich and a Jew would receive but scant mercy at the hands of the prejudiced master.

But, although the opinions of Wagner, however deeply they may be disfigured by bias, cannot be lightly set aside, we have no hesitation in pronouncing them unjust in at least one respect. For even those who most differ from the tendency of Meyerbeer cannot—if they be just—for a moment deny that he was a musician possessed of great gifts. Indeed, had it been otherwise, the outcry against him would have been less pronounced. A less capable man might have escaped obloquy for works which were in accordance with his lights. With Meyerbeer it is undisputed genius frittered away in undignified subservience to unworthy motives which his detractors condemn.

The son of rich parents, cradled in luxury that ever remained at his beck and call, the boy gave early promise of musical talent. As a mere child he had the faculty of repeating melodies correctly after a first hearing. There was no attempt to stifle his talent. The best of teachers were engaged. Lauska, considered at the head of his profession in Berlin, superintended his studies; and the aged Clementi was so delighted with his aptitude that he gave him lessons during the whole of his stay. As a boy of nine, Meyerbeer performed at a concert, and was rapturously applauded. In 1806 he joined the private academy of Vogler of Darmstadt, who has been variously pronounced

an excellent authority and an egregious charlatan. One of his co-disciples, the celebrated
Weber, became bound to him in friendship that
only ceased with his death.

In Meyerbeer's early compositions church
music predominates. An opera, *Jephthah's Vow*,
singularly dry and heavy, and altogether more
like an oratorio, was performed at Munich, and
not appreciated by the public, though connois-
seurs thought highly of it. This is the case
with all his earlier music, and points to the fact
that the subsequent idol of the crowd started
as a caterer to exclusive tastes.

In 1813 he wrote the comic opera, *Abimelek*,
performed with some success at Stuttgart and
Prague. A journey to Vienna, undertaken in
order to superintend its performance at that
city, brought him face to face with Hummel,
whose execution as a pianist threw him into
such raptures that he postponed all his plans
for the moment with the object of perfect-
ing his own play. Moscheles, who heard him
at that time, said that, 'had he persevered,
as a pianist he would have had few equals.'
But his mind was set on composing, and even
at that early age his thirst for popularity
was evident. The comparative failure of his
opera at Vienna plunged him into the deepest

grief, and did much to determine his future career.

After a brief stay in Paris he went to Italy, with the ambitious intention to beard the all-powerful Rossini in his lair. The imitative powers of Meyerbeer which enabled him to identify himself at the shortest notice with any style stood him in good stead. In Italy he composed operas so thoroughly Italian, that all his German training seemed to have evaporated into space. The success was instantaneous. The laurels of Rossini seemed for a moment to pale beside the daring assault of this audacious youngster. *Il Crociato*, his best creation during that period, electrified the audience at Venice, and nothing would satisfy them until the master had made his bow from the stage and accepted a wreath tendered him.

Emboldened by this triumph he had the opera performed at Berlin, but in Germany they would have none of Italian music, and in Paris the result was not much better. From 1825-1831 very little is heard of the composer. The death of his father, followed by the death of two of his children, saddened the feelings of this man who was thoroughly typical of his race in his strong family attachments. These bereavements, coupled with the growing disapprobation of his friends at his musical aberrations, brought about the momentous decision, not only to expatriate himself from the land with which he was no longer in artistic touch, but, moreover, to desert the Italian for the French style of music.

Auber and Boieldieu had been his precursors in paving the way for a national opera which was to hold the mean between the pure reign of melody, to the exclusion of dramatic exigencies which obtained in Italy, and the prevalence of harmony characteristic of German opera. The French masters, while refusing to tie themselves down strictly to the dictates of the *libretto*, introduced a style which has been aptly described as 'decorative' music. There, opera becomes a series of tableaux set off by music, which, like the scenery, the costumes, and the general arrangement, took the place of an accessory rather than that of the principal part. The impressionable character of the French lent itself easily to a tendency which aimed at startling effect rather than gradual development. This function Meyerbeer proposed to amplify, and render so effective that, without impairing the principle laid down by Auber, the music should by means fair or foul be expressive of effects so thrilling that the enthusiasm of the audience should be taken by storm.   The stupendous crescendos, worked up by all the resources of orchestra, largely reinforced at his instigation, until the house shakes with the culminating *fortissimo*, the whole augmented by startling scenery, exciting action, and the weird stage effects producible only on the grandest of theatres, and sufficiently familiar to frequenters of Meyerbeer's *repertoire* to need comment.

To qualify himself for this task the master locked himself up for years, and undertook studies of French history, French music, French taste, so comprehensive that even his laborious habits must have been subjected to no ordinary strain to master the piles of books and manuscripts that crowded his library.

At last he was ready, and the result stood revealed. *Robert le Diable* and the *Huguenots* are operas so intensely descriptive of French history and French customs, so irresistibly appealing to the fancies of the excitable Gauls, that it is not surprising they should have landed him from comparative obscurity by one bound into the first place in the heart of the audience. The success was instantaneous, and even in Germany these operas and the subsequent ones, *Le Prophète* and *Dinorah*, held the boards in spite of the frantic opposition of the classical school. As early as 1852 the performances in Paris alone had reached 100 of the *Prophète*, 222 of the *Huguenots*, and 330 of *Robert*, figures which in those days were nearly incredible. There were not wanting critics who pronounced Meyerbeer the greatest composer ever known or ever likely to exist, and the Prussian Government, proud of its brilliant subject, and anxious to secure his services, recalled him to Berlin in the most flattering terms, and with the title of Royal Kapellmeister.

There is ample evidence of his activity during the time he held that position. Though never a great leader of orchestra he deserved well of the Berlin opera. *Euryanthe*, by Weber, was put on the boards as a sacred legacy bequeathed by his dead friend, and Wagner ought at least to have remembered that, if his opera *Rienzi* was performed at Berlin in spite of previous failure, this was solely due to the master whom he could not sufficiently revile. The *Feldlager in Schlesien*, composed by Meyerbeer for Berlin, had a moderate success, and *Struensee*, written to a drama by his brother, though scarcely known, is considered by many to be his best work.

In 1849 he returned to Paris, which was after

all his most appreciative soil. The *Prophète*, just completed, was performed with phenomenal success. His last years call for little mention. The *North Star* (into which were merged some melodies from the *Feldlager in Schlesien*) and *Dinorah* were among his last compositions, excepting the *Africaine*, on which he had worked off and on for over thirty years. Racked by painful diseases and compelled to have frequent recourse to watering-places, he yet worked to the last with unabated energy. A march and hymn for the accession of William I. of Prussia give evidence that his connection with the country of his birth had not ceased. On the 2nd May 1864 he breathed his last. He was not spared to see the performance of his *Africaine*, which took place in 1865. To all his works he had devoted the most minute care, changing and substituting up to the hour of performance, but on none more so than on this favourite child of his brain. Though no expression to that effect is on record, it may, we think, be assumed that he thought it his best opera, but this opinion was not shared by the public, who prefer *Robert*, and, above all, the *Huguenots*.

That Meyerbeer's music, besides many passages of sublime grandeur, contains much that is trivial and reprehensible, few will deny. Some of his arias opening with heroic majesty subside with paltry endings, rendered the more feeble by contrast with the preceding strains, rung forth by the premier voices of the day with all the powerful adjuncts of orchestral effect. His successes were eminently popular ; he spared no pains to hire enemies into his camp and disarm the sting of hostile criticism ; but music is an aristocratic art, and if the claims of Bach and Beethoven were submitted to universal suffrage they would come off badly indeed. Impartial observers must therefore side with those of Meyerbeer's opponents who regret that a great genius has been unworthily employed. What strengthens their case even more is the fact that he spared no money to enhance his successes by such despicable means as a paid *claque*, bribed journalists, and heavy bets, so framed as to artificially crowd out other operas in favour of his own. Of all the hundreds of thousands which were made out of his operas hardly anything flowed into his pockets ; but this cannot be put down to disinterestedness, as his private fortune counted by millions, and he could well afford to gratify any desires he might have for publicity.

For all that he was a very modest man, and

no harsh or overbearing word is reported of him. With most of his contemporaries he lived on good terms ; towards Rossini he behaved with a submission more than remarkable, and the Italian master held him in great esteem, and was much shocked at the news of his death. An insatiable craving for popularity is responsible for most of the faults imputed to him. He was well known in Paris, and much gratified when passers-by remarked, ' *Voilà M. Meyerbeer !* ' It is said that the reproduction of his melodies on the vilest of barrel-organs elicited a contented smile. Ever in seach of dormant talent, the world is probably indebted to him for the proper development of many famous singers, notably Lucca, and, in a measure, for Jenny Lind.

As a last word, let us not forget that the poor and needy seldom applied to him in vain. The *Meyerbeer Stiftung* in Berlin, and many similar bequests, bear testimony to the goodness of his heart.

MOZART

1756-1791

IN all the variegated annals of musical heroes, not one is to be found whose life has been replete with triumphs so signal, opposed to reverses so cruel, as those reserved for the subject of this chapter. The early promise of childhood was more than borne out by the most phenomenal of creations in later days. But, unfortunately, the brilliant achievements of genius and patience did not serve to shield their author from the petty annoyances of everyday life; even from the pangs of hunger and privation ; which, though they could not obscure his splendid powers, drove him into an early and unknown grave. With deep emotion and sincere reverence we approach the tale of unexampled misery meted out to a character exquisitely lovable and unblemished ; misfortunes enhanced in an eminent degree by its childlike simplicity and total absence of worldliness.

Mozart was born at Salzburg on the 30th June 1756. His father, a man of sound musical training, was possessed of excellent common sense.   The boy Wolfgang and a sister, five years his senior, who as ' Nannerl ' occupies so great a space in his little heart, were the only surviving children out of seven.

When Nannerl received her first musical instruction, it was noticed that the brother, a baby of three years of age, would forget his playthings and steal up to her side, lost in rapturous attention.   When the lesson was over, he would pass his little fingers over the keys, and overbrim into exaggerated expressions of childish delight when he struck a consonance. These proofs of an uncommon talent were of such frequent recurrence that they could not be put down to accident.   After a time the boy would repeat simple melodies after one or two hearings ; very soon, and before knowing the notes, he began to extemporise little pieces, remarkable for their correct har- ᐟmony.   Indeed, his sensitiveness to dissonance was so keen that a harsh and jarring discord would bring the tears to his eyes, and the sound of a trumpet make him faint.   As a boy of four he played with taste and feeling.   The father, afraid of overstraining the child at this tender age, did everything to repress his eagerness, but could not succeed in keeping him from the piano.   There he would sit for

hours at a time playing and improvising. His
eyes were lit up by a strange fire, his face was
serious beyond his years. While so employed,
a joke, however innocent, would pain him ; the
only remark habitual to him was the question
addressed to his wondering audience : ' Do you
love me ? ' It was no idle question.; it was the
emotion with which his heart was overflowing,
the nourishment of which, more than others, his
tender mind was ever in need. Perchance, at
times, some one would tease him by saying ' no,'
but they would soon repent this harmless joke
when they saw the tears start to the boy's eyes.
Of love and of music the child's soul was
composed ; to love and be loved was the key-
note of his existence. Alas that it should have
remained so, only to become the cause of all
his misfortunes !

In other respects he was just like any child
of his age, gay and boisterous, as far as his
delicate health would admit, fond of play and
passionately devoted to those around him. It
was only at the piano that he assumed the
solemn air which showed that music was to
him something widely removed from play.
And the character of his works points to the
fact that, if ever music was inspiration divine,
it was so in his case. Even while playing and

romping it was ever uppermost in his thoughts. The removal of his playthings from one room to another had to be effected to the strains of a march, and similar incidents are plentifully dispersed over his early history. Parents and sister, dearly beloved by the little fellow, doted on him. Never had he been to them aught but a source of unmixed joy ; punishment was unknown to him, his docile temper did not call for it, and the effects on a nervous temperament so highly strung might have been serious. In after years the father related that they had often regarded him with secret fear ; so delicate and gifted a child, they thought, would not attain manhood.

In 1762, the boy being six years of age, the first journey was undertaken. At Munich the children played before the Elector, and the result was so encouraging that the trip was extended to Vienna. At this town a perfect ovation awaited the family. The scenes that were enacted day by day at court had never been known in the Imperial palace, with its stiff unbending etiquette. The Emperor forgot the dignity of his position, and subjected himself to treatment which would have fairly shocked some of his ceremonious ancestors. The Empress, a model of true womanliness, a

rare embodiment of chaste wife- and mother-
hood, in that age of licentious corruption, was
never tired of caressing that most lovable of
children, who addressed her by the familiar
' Du,' who made her lap his home, and whose
kisses knew not of the trammels of rank and
the worship of a throne.   The little Archduchesses were to him brothers and sisters, with
whom he might romp through the splendid
rooms, blissfully ignorant in the democracy of
childhood of what is due to Imperial Highnesses,
and the ladies, taking their cue from their superiors, lost their hearts to the fascinating little
fellow.   Had it not been for the scarlet fever,
which at this important juncture cut short his connection with the court, his life might have been
cast in different lines ; but the fear of infection
made him suddenly an object to be shunned,
and aided the short-lived memory of the great
to expunge a strange intermezzo from the cold
and measured routine of every-day life.

However, the child's triumphs were by no
means over.   At Versailles a repetition of the
Vienna experience took place, and in London
the music-loving - Royal Family showed the
greatest interest in the infant prodigy.   The
first published compositions, printed and dedicated to Madame Victoire, the daughter of

L

Louis XV., date from that journey; they were
shortly followed by six sonatas, dedicated to
the Queen of England.   But even at this early
period of unparalleled triumph we find the
father complaining that the financial results are
not commensurate.   'If we could only change
a few of those kisses into coin!' is his constant
refrain; 'we have watches and snuff-boxes
enough to stock a jeweller's establishment, but
no money!' and even the boy joins in in his
quaint childish way.   He wants to have
watches hanging out of each of his pockets to
show kind-hearted donors that he has no
further need of that article!

All this time the musical capacities of the
boy are increasing apace, and the concerts at
which he appears are almost exclusively made
up of his own compositions.   After a stay of
over one year in England the family leave for
Holland, greatly impeded by illness which over-
takes both Wolfgang and his sister.   The success at the court of the Prince of Orange is no
less phenomenal, but at Paris, which is their
next stage, the performances seem to fall flat,
and the first warning note is sounded that
precocious reputations are rarely long-lived.
The home voyage *via* Switzerland is mainly
remarkable for an unsuccessful attempt to visit

Voltaire, who was ill. The meeting between the straitlaced and most orthodox Mozart père and the sceptical *écraseur* of the *infâme* would have been a splendid subject for a *genre* painter.

The arrival at Salzburg is the signal for a course of severe study, welcome food to the boy's insatiable appetite. The *rôle* as infant phenomenon is now definitively cast aside; henceforth the tenderness in years must be disguised rather than accentuated. The time has come to enter into competition with the elders, and for this purpose the world considers youth a disadvantage and something to be regarded with suspicion. Already jealousy rears her ugly head, and bad luck begins to dog the footsteps of the youthful master. The death of the Emperor, sincerely mourned by his widow, and the inauguration with the advent of Joseph II. of a reign of frugality and parsimony, eagerly imitated by a number of sycophants, is not favourable to Mozart's desire to obtain employment.

Nevertheless the kindly Emperor commissions him to write an opera, and selects for this purpose the libretto *La Finta Semplice*. This opera was never performed. The Italian clique, all powerful at Court, resented the pretension of a boy of eleven, and the orchestra refused roundly to be led by one so youthful. Greatly mortified and unable to obtain an engagement at Vienna he returns to Salzburg. He has the joy to see his rejected opera placed on the boards, and receives the appointment as concert-master to the Archbishop, but this purely honorary title does not provide him with the means of existence of which he stands in need.

Since the fame legitimately achieved is still insufficient, the father determines to have recourse to the *ultima ratio* of those days. In 1769 he starts with his son for Italy. The fame of the lad has preceded him, but it is regarded with suspicion and incredulity. Such things as boy musicians have been known before ; they have seldom out-lasted their childhood. The first serious task placed before them generally proves a sharp extinguisher to these ephemeral reputations. Let Mozart come ; they will soon find out the weak points in his armour. They place the tasks before him ; as child's-play they are solved—solved in a manner which adepts, aged in the study of music, have never dreamt of. They search for fresh problems ; wise professors put their heads together to devise some formula profound enough to baffle this German stripling. It is in vain. In two Italian cities he is elected member of philharmonic societies, not without hesitation, not before the most cruel of doubts have been expressed and vanquished. His father is supposed to have helped him—by some underhand means he has procured the key to the problems placed before him. 'Very well, then,' he exclaims, 'give me fresh problems ; lock me up and set a watch on my movements while I work them out !' It is done as he desires. At last doubt becomes impossible ; suspicion changes into enthusiasm ; old abbés blanched in the worship of Mercadante, and who have long. become reconciled to the conviction that Palestrina and Allegri have scaled the last rung of the ladder of musical genius, beyond which there is no ascent, are compelled to admit that a master has arisen destined to eclipse everything that has hitherto been seen or heard. '*Evviva il maestro, evviva il maestrino!*' is the shout heard from one end of the art-loving peninsula to the other, and wherever Mozart plants his foot, new and unheard-of musical feats proclaim that his star, far from paling, is still in the ascendant, that the downward turn is as far off as ever, that what he offers to the world is no empty trick of legerdemain, no exposition of ephemeral pyrotechnics, but the true impress of genius, the like of which surpasses all imagination.

At Rome the celebrated *Miserere* of Allegri is performed. So sacred is the possession of this masterpiece held, that the score is jealously kept under lock and key. No copy of it is allowed to be taken. Rome alone is to be possessed of the acme of sacred music; no other city may be permitted to rob the capital of the ancient world of its exclusive privilege. But the framers of this wise precaution did not bargain for the memory of a Mozart. To hear the mass once and write it down from memory, a feat impossible to others, is not so to him. The Pope hears of it and doubts; nothing but the examination of the score will satisfy him. Competent men inform him that the rumour is only too true, and then he sends for Mozart. The Order of the Golden Spur is the mark of his appreciation. Gluck has received this decoration when in the zenith of his fame, and ever since he has called himself the Chevalier Gluck. Not so the boy; he takes the bauble but never uses it, and continues to call himself by a name immeasurably more honoured by posterity, that of simple Wolfgang Amadeus Mozart.

Three operas and a large number of other compositions may be traced to this Italian visit; for two years in succession his was the

opera which received the place of honour at the
Milan Carnival. Hundreds of anecdotes, many
of which are, no doubt, spurious, bear testimony
to the brilliancy of his achievements, and to the
irresistible way in which he battled down prejudices and doubts which assailed him from all
sides.

His voyage had been interrupted by the in-
stallation of a new Archbishop of Salzburg in
1772, for which occasion he composed a cantata.
But in spite of his brilliant successes his application for the post of Kapellmeister was refused.
The prophet counts for nothing in his fatherland. Three long and weary years he waits
patiently; then, reluctantly, he leaves home in
search of the modest pittance denied him
Munich is his first stage; there his memory is
still honoured; there he may hope to find a
lasting home. It is no great wage he asks at
the hands of the Elector—500 florins (equal to
forty pounds); and for this he is willing to compose four operas, and to play at court every
day. 'He is too young,' is the reply; 'let him
go to Italy and make his name, then I shall not
refuse.' Go to Italy and make a name? He
has been there and who has made a greater
name. 'Will your Highness call together all
the best composers that I may compete with

them ?   I ask nothing better.'   No, his Highness will not do so, and the poor lad has to leave Munich, deified by the public but unable to obtain the appreciation of Princes, which alone in those days could be of use to him.

At Augsburg he gives a concert to defray his travelling expenses.   'Never,' he writes to his father, 'have I received greater applause!' But beyond the applause ninety florins is all he obtains.   At Mannheim he is well received, but there is no vacancy.   There is no help, he has to try Paris again ; but at Paris he fares no better.   A libretto that he is promised never arrives, and at last, after months of vain plead- ing and bitter disappointment, he is glad to find a pupil who is generous enough to pay him three louis for twelve lessons.   'If I only knew here of ears to listen, a heart to feel, and the faintest understanding for music, I should feel happy in spite of all my reverses,' he writes in the depth of despair.   For years after the bitter memories of Paris haunt his mind.   And now a blow befalls him, the bitterest he has yet known ; the mother, whom he has worshipped with all the tenderness of his heart, dies sud- denly.

In 1779, twenty-three years of age, one of the greatest musicians the world has seen esteems

himself lucky to obtain a position as organist
to the court, and afterwards to the cathedral of
Salzburg, at a salary scarcely sufficient to defray
the most rudimentary expenses of living.   That
his splendid genius did not only survive but
rise superior to these continual reverses is, in
itself, a proof of its irresistible vigour.   A call
to Munich, during 1780, may have occurred to
him as somewhat of a relenting of his bitter
ill-fortune.   If so, it was doomed to disappointment, although it gave him occasion to compose the most memorable work he had yet
attempted.

The opera, *Idomeneo*, which was received with
unbounded success by the public, and vindicated
for its composer, at the hands of his confrères,
the title of the greatest musician of his time,
constitutes an entirely new departure in operatic
music.   The style is so essentially original, so
divergent from anything hitherto known in Italy,
Germany, or France, and so anticipatory of ideas
that were to obtain much later, that competent
judges have pronounced it the origin of all new
opera.   It may appear surprising that a work
so eminently subversive of all tradition should
have met with immediate recognition; yet such
was undoubtedly the case.   The name of
Mozart was again wafted across the whole

extent of the musical world. It must have seemed as if this success would at last carry him into a safe harbour. Twenty years sooner it would probably have done so, but the time in which he flourished was one of reaction and severe retrenchment.

His master, the Archbishop of Salzburg, not unwilling to partake of the glory the possession of such a genius might shed over his person, took him to Vienna, where he had to board and lodge with the servants and put up with the most galling insults. The eminent dispenser of Christian grace and benevolence was not above torturing his unfortunate dependant to the top of his bent. For a long time poor Mozart submitted to being the butt of his delicate humour. 'Gutter boy, villain, low fellow, Lump,' and similar terms of endearment, were by no means sparingly inserted in his conversation. If Mozart had had himself alone to consider, he would probably have cut short the connection long before he did, but there was the position of his father to be taken into account, and the prelate made no secret of his intention to visit the supposed sins of the son on the father. At last, however, things became unbearable, and the breach, long impending, took effect in a way which admitted of no reconciliation. 'Is your grace dissatisfied with me?' timidly askes the composer, mindful of his father struggling at Salzburg. In reply he is literally kicked out of the palace, and thus terminates this most unfortunate of engagements.

For over a year Mozart, landed on the pavement of Vienna, was dependent for his living on what he could make out of lessons and the sale of compositions. The Emperor Joseph, well meaning but surrounded by a strong cabal of intriguing Italians, and honestly devoted to their style, could not appreciate his great subject. All the influence of some great ladies at court had to be employed to procure him a commission to compose an opera. The *Entführung aus dem Serail* which was the work in question was coldly received in Vienna, while throughout Germany it met with such signal success that at last even the prejudiced Viennese circles found it wise to bury their prejudices. 'There are too many notes in the opera,' was the Emperor's verdict. 'Not more nor less than required,' was the answer, which did not, however, increase the favour in which the composer was held. Fifty ducats for the opera, and— much later—a salary of eight hundred florins as composer to the court, were all the emoluments Mozart's friends could procure from his apathetic sovereign, and to make these eight hundred florins appear in the light of an alms, the court for years deliberately abstained from availing itself of his services, with the exception of the little opera, *Der Schauspieldirector*, performed in 1786. 'Too much for what I am set to do and too little for what I could do,' is the sad remark wrung from Mozart with regard to this salary.   It is the opinion of C. M. von Weber, that no opera can compare with the *Entführung* for placid sweetness of melody and beauty of instrumentation ; he does not even except the later and more successful works by the same composer.   The sweet influence of love at this time exercised its potent sway over the composer.   There are many chance coincidences between the plot of the opera and the troubled course of his love romance.   The name of the heroine, Constanze, was also that of his bride, and whereas the plot of the opera turns on an elopement, he himself had to resort to this drastic remedy to obtain what he hoped would be his happiness.

It was not his first encounter with Cupid. A previous love affair with the gifted singer Aloysia Weber had thrown his father into great consternation.   It had been responsible for a longer stay at Mannheim than would otherwise have been called for. But at last it had been broken off, partly through fickleness on the part of the girl, partly through a severe exercise of his father's authority. It was the only occasion on which something like a cloud threatened to obscure the hearty relations between father and son. The former, ever solicitous for the son's fame, deprecated marriage, especially when coupled with impecuniosity. Wolfgang, he thought, should be wedded to his art only. 'Come back instantly!' one of his letters runs, 'it is folly to saddle yourself with a wife and children, doomed possibly to ruin and starvation.' Was there foreknowledge in this sombre prophecy, which the composer at the time regarded as well-meant exaggeration, but which was fulfilled to the letter? It did not influence his decision ; when has love been amenable to the dictates of common-sense? But the paternal displeasure was a thing not to be set aside lightly, and he resolved to cut short all opposition by taking the bull by the horns. When Leopold Mozart was made aware of his son's decision, it was too late to remonstrate. The bond uniting him to Constanze Weber, the sister of his first faithless love, had already been sealed, and nothing remained but vain regret and an estrangement which lasted for years.

Thus commenced a marriage which was productive of some happiness alloyed by great misery. The girl, though fondly attached to her husband, was just as inexperienced in worldly wisdom, and instead of buoying him up with that counsel which his improvident nature stood in need of, she added to the hopeless confusion which rendered the household a purgatory peopled by exasperated creditors and importunate duns, and often devoid of the barest necessities of life.

Wherever we glance we are confronted by the saddening spectacle of the destruction that can be wrought upon a nature weak and confiding, that has never emerged from childhood. And yet, though ill-luck was largely responsible for the melancholy state of affairs, though the most energetic of tempers must get warped by the continued sting of indifference, as inexplicable as it was undeserved, there can be no doubt that, if properly husbanded, his resources, however meagre, ought to have sufficed for a small and unpretentious household. Had Mozart as a teacher applied himself to those of his pupils who, though incapable as musicians, were yet able to pay for their lessons, instead of lavishing his pains on those who both as regards talents and impecuniosity approached nearer to his own standard, the result would have been more gratifying to his pocket and his happiness. Had he sold his compositions instead of giving them away to unworthy associates, who traded on his good-nature; had he shunned such of them as, under the pretext of a loan, unscrupulously bargained the productions of his brain to publishers, who with the perspicacity of vultures scented the booty from afar; had he locked up his scores instead of letting them lie about the room a prey to the dustbin and the fire hearth, it would doubtless have sufficed to pay for the bread and butter. But the inborn good-nature of the composer, absolute in its disinterestedness, culpable in its indiscrimination, untempered alike by his own heartrending indigence and the most crying distress of his family, unable to refuse aught to an enemy, and culminating in a childlike fidelity to a sovereign whose claims to his gratitude we fail to perceive, proved his ruin, and show to the world the strange and pitiable spectacle of a genius weighed down by the most trivial miseries of everyday life, until an early grave lies yawning before him.

But while the gnawing tooth of poverty is preying on his vitals, while enemies rise up in legion against the most unoffending of beings, while the obstinacy of the court in disregarding the claims of its most devoted and illustrious servitor seems to increase in proportion as the public voice is raised in his favour, his genius finds expression in works which stand unrivalled to this day. It is impossible to enumerate the scores that issue from his pen with the fluency of magic. Suffice it to say that, not allowing for the number of compositions lost and uncompleted, the number of complete works left by Mozart exceeds nine hundred, of which the overwhelming portion is traceable to those eleven years of unrelieved penury that are identified with his sojourn in Vienna.

The year 1785 is memorable for the magnificent cantata, *Davidde Penitente*, which ought to be more widely known. Six quartets, dedicated to Haydn, ' from whom he has learnt to write quartets,' bear a touching testimony to his modesty, and the affection which linked these two eminent men together. Of all the composers of that fertile age, Haydn, who nearest approached the fame of his young contemporary, was yet the only one to recognise fully and unreservedly his superior genius. ' Upon my honour and before God, I declare that your son is the first composer of our time,'

the old master says to Leopold Mozart, unheeding the greater measure of success which
seemed to pronounce the award of merit and
fame in his own favour.

Le Nozze di Figaro follows in 1786. This
marvellous work, the brightness of which is
difficult to reconcile with the gloomy life and
failing health of the composer, is second in
popularity to *Don Giovanni* only, while in
musical value it is widely considered superior
to the latter opera. To obtain the Emperor's
consent for the composition of this opera was
no easy matter. 'Mozart cannot compose
opera' was his constant refrain; and, when at
last all obstacles had been removed, the Italian
singers, intent on wrecking the opera, sang so
badly that Mozart appealed for protection to
the Emperor. The second performance was
better, but it was evident that Vienna was
prejudiced against his music. A new opera
by Martini, *La Cosa Rara*, made short work of
Figaro; the divine creation of Mozart was
laughingly shelved in favour of Martini's composition! Who knows now of Martini, and
who of *La Cosa Rara*? By a singular infatua-
tion the great composers of the greatest musical era have made Vienna their home, and
thus invested that city with a halo of musical

M

romance to which it has little claim. Indeed, we should say that Vienna is famed for the number of celebrated composers whom it has deliberately ignored and allowed to starve!

But if the metropolis turned its back on its most illustrious inhabitant, there was no want of appreciation in other cities. At Prague, *Figaro* was performed with such unbounded success that the composer promised to write his next opera for that city. This proved to be the most celebrated of all his works, *Don Giovanni*, which to this day is second in popularity to no opera, ancient or modern. *Don Giovanni* was a revelation; it uprooted opera in its very foundation. From the most extravagant gaiety to extreme pathos hardly an imaginable emotion is unrepresented, and the music is so appropriate, the harmony so exquisite, that the most severe of critics have stood silent before the perfection of its structure. That the overture was written on the night before the performance and played by the orchestra at first sight is well known, but not so remarkable as the general *ensemble* of the whole opera, the masterly blending of libretto and music, and the care bestowed by Mozart on the elaboration of the plot, which proves that besides his own musical qualities he stood possessed of great dramatic gifts. Again Vienna society proved its inanity; the work, regarding the supreme merit of which there was only one voice, fell flat in the capital, and was superseded by Salieri's *Axur*.

Some meagre recognition was, however, now conveyed by the appointment as Imperial court composer, with a salary of eight hundred florins, above referred to. The edict dates from 1789, and though it did not materially improve the straitened circumstances of the composer, it laid him unfortunately under a debt of gratitude, and gave him soon the melancholy opportunity to prove his doglike fidelity to a master who had certainly done nothing to deserve it.

Illness and melancholy are now crowding around the master's couch, foreshadowing the end which was soon to come. But the more reason there is to rest his aching brain, the more feverish his activity becomes. The fear, often expressed, that he would leave the world without having done sufficient for his glory, gains hold of him with irrepressible force. The prayers of his wife, most loving and anxious of nurses, the commands of his doctor, remain unheeded. Late into the dismal night he sits, pencil in hand, poring over manuscripts into which he has infused the life-blood of his inspiration. The incomparable symphonies in C, E flat, and G minor, take shape under the trembling fingers of the pale-faced master, wasting away under the inexorable ravages of broken health and heart. *Cosi Fan Tutte*, perhaps inferior to his more famous operas, and yet sparkling with wit and humour, is one of the pain-gotten children of this last year but one. The adaptation of some of Handel's oratorios to increased orchestral accompaniment is a labour of love. But every now and then the sordid necessities of everyday life drive him from Vienna to places where his works find more generous appreciation.

Nowhere is his name held in greater honour than in Berlin. The art-loving king receives him with the greatest distinction. Here, at least, is one who values Mozart according to his merits; here is a prospect which to one less unpractical might have meant life and happiness.

'How do you like my orchestra?' the king inquires.

'It is good, your Majesty,' answers Mozart; 'and yet there is room for improvement.'

'Stay with me, then, as Kapellmeister. You shall have three thousand thalers a year.'

The tears rise to Mozart's eyes. He doubts his ears. Should there after all be somebody in the world willing to appreciate him? Three thousand thalers—why, it is eight times the amount he receives from His most gracious Majesty of Vienna. But only one moment does he hesitate before he replies.

'I thank your Majesty from the bottom of my heart, but how can I leave my Kaiser?'

'Well, well,' the King replies, touched by such devotion, 'you may consider the offer. It remains open.'

He travels back *via* Leipzig. In that town he meets Doles, the favourite pupil of Bach. With characteristic modesty he pauses before he passes his fingers over the keys of the organ which has resounded under those revered fingers. 'Thank God, there is at last a worthy successor to Johann Sebastian!' is the judgment of Doles. During the long weary drive to Vienna he may have thought often of the splendid offer of the Prussian monarch; it must have contrasted with the misery in wait for him. For the journey has not been a financial success. 'You must be satisfied with *me*,' he writes to his Constance, 'and not ask for money.' We can imagine the pressure of friends, when informed of the munificent offer, to discard a sentimentality which is uncalled for, foolish—nay, even culpable ; we cannot feel angry with Frau Constanze if she has reminded her spouse of the duty he owes herself and her children, since he will insist on disregarding his own claims.   At last his scruples are overcome.   He tenders his resignation.

'I cannot make my living in Vienna,' he says to his Kaiser.

But the latter knows his man.   Although even now he cannot appreciate him, it dawns on his Imperial mind that there must be something in Mozart which provokes the enthusiasm reigning everywhere but in the good city of Vienna.

'And you can leave me, Mozart?' is his reply.

That is too much for the unlucky possessor of a childlike heart.

'No, your Majesty,' he replies.   'I cannot leave you, I must stay.'

Weak and blameable! the strong-minded among our readers will exclaim.   One so stupid deserves his fate.   We must plead guilty to this indictment.   No man would have acted thus ; but then, Mozart was no man, he was never more than a child, and in matters pertaining to money and worldliness, a child among children.

'At least you have insisted on an increase of pay,' his friends ask when informed of this latest act of Quixotism.

'How could I?' he answers. 'At such a moment!'

And the Imperial patron never intimates a desire to reward the fidelity he has not hesitated to appeal to. Joseph II. was one of the worthiest monarchs that have ever graced a throne. Liberal to the core, his desire was to promote reforms for the welfare of his people, and their ingratitude, which imputed to him motives entirely foreign to his nature, drove him into an early grave. We are sorry to record of a sovereign so admirable, an action which the staunchest of his adherents cannot defend.

And now we come to the last year of the composer's life, the climax of struggles and trials preceding the final act of the drama. Again he makes a bid for the favour of the ungrateful town; again he is refused. The functions of a second Kapellmeister are considered beyond the capabilities of a Mozart; he has to content himself with the place of an unpaid assistant to the organist of St. Stephen's. While his health is sinking fast, and his circumstances are worse than ever, Schikaneder, a ruined theatrical manager, applies to him to compose the *Magic Flute*. 'What is your price?' he asks the composer, whose wan face speaks of starvation. 'Since you are poor yourself,' he replies, 'I must leave that to you, provided I have the right to produce the opera elsewhere.' 'Agreed,' says Schikaneder, and proceeds forthwith to sell the opera in all places where he can find a market. 'Will you not take action against him?' ask Mozart's friends. 'No,' he replies, 'he is a rascal.'

This opera proves the greatest financial success of any of Mozart's works. Schikaneder penniless and bankrupt, becomes a rich man, while his dupe is hurrying towards his pauper grave. *La Clemenza di Tito* is his last operatic composition. It marks the accession of the new Emperor, Leopold, who has no sympathy with music of any kind.

And now, while the death angel is hovering around his prey, there remains to be told that strange and weird history of the Requiem, pathetically illustrative of the unfinished life of its sublime composer. In all the annals of music we seek in vain for a tale more heart-rending, an issue more sad than the mysterious circumstances which link together the expiring days of the composer and the death mass which filled his entire mind—a last grim battle between Death and Genius.

An unknown man commissions the master to write a Requiem. He pays the price demanded and stipulates a time at which he may call for the score. Ill and melancholy, Mozart works night and day, but the time expires and the work is unfinished. A second time the mysterious visitor appears. Will he grant an extension of time? Yes, as much as the composer desires. Again the strange messenger disappears. And now the health of Mozart becomes alarmingly worse, but yet he works with an assiduity that excludes all other thought from his mind. An irresistible fascination seems to rivet him to that score, while his brain is racked with fever and his pulse runs riot. His wife, anxious and tormented, consults the doctor. The score must be hidden away, is the verdict, but the composer frets and worries. Life is intolerable to him without this occupation. 'Do you not comprehend?' he asks petulantly. 'The messenger who ordered this work is sent from heaven. It is my own death chant I am writing.' They give him back the score, and forthwith he buries himself in this all-engrossing task. Work and fainting fits, fainting fits and work, constitute the last days of the unfortunate man. The mass is nearing its completion and yet he feels that he will not complete it. A rehearsal is held of the parts written ; he himself in a weak tremulous voice sings the alto part, but when they come to the *Lacrimosa* he breaks down. 'O God! that I should be denied the boon to finish this work!' he cries in impotent despair.

The fainting fits now increase in vigour ; for hours at a time he lies prostrate, and the lucid intervals are taken up by work and instruction to his pupil Süssmayer regarding the unfinished portions. Meanwhile the *Zauberflöte* is playing to ever-increasing audiences. Unheard of is the success ; it gladdens the heart of the composer, lying on his deathbed and unable to wield the bâton and drink in that applause which so long has been denied him by the Viennese. The watch is in his hands, and in thought he follows the course of the opera. Now this aria is being sung, now the chorus is approaching. At last his fame has broken through its trammels. Now, when it is too late, Vienna offers him the bâton of Kapellmeister which he has applied for in vain. A powerful syndicate of noblemen club together to offer him an ample annuity. From Amsterdam proposals are submitted which will place him above need for the rest of his days. But he is travelling now post-haste to a country where annuities are of no avail.

On the evening of the 4th December he is still occupied giving Süssmayer instructions regarding the score. A fainting fit interrupts him. It was to be his last. At midnight he sits up in bed with his eyes fixed on the ceiling, and then turns around to the wall as if asleep. At one o'clock of the 5th his spirit passes away.

His last malady seems to have been typhoid fever. The funeral took place on the next day. It is a pauper's coffin and in a pauper's grave. A storm is raging, and alone the corpse arrives at the cemetery and is interred with several others in a pauper's vault. His widow, stricken down with illness, has been unable to cheer his last moments. When, hardly recovered, she goes to the graveyard to pray on his grave, it cannot be traced! As if all powers had combined to efface from the world the relics of one whom it had neglected while he was yet mingled with the living, the grave-digger, who alone could have given information, had died two days after Mozart's funeral! Thus ended the life of one of the most divinely gifted among men.

In appearance Mozart was short and delicate,

188 THE GREAT COMPOSERS

with regular features and beautiful eyes of un-
fathomable depth and intensity. He was fond
of dancing and skittles, and a good mathema-
tician. At billiards he is said to have been
exceedingly good. Detractors have tried to
fasten on him the reproach of intemperance.
We seek in vain for any confirmation of this
statement, and, looking at the enormous quantity
of his work, it is most unlikely that he should
have been a drunkard ; that at times he enjoyed a glass of wine is quite possible.

The place of Mozart in the world of music
requires no comment. That he was one of the
greatest masters ever known is now no longer
disputed ; indeed, in the opinion of authorities
so widely divergent in style as Chopin, Gounod,
Wagner, he is the absolutely greatest.

Numerous attempts have been made to
adjust the respective claims of Mozart and
Beethoven, but we think it absolutely impossible
to draw a parallel between two men who have
both attained to eminence, but each in a per-
fectly different style of music. No more can
Raphael be classed with Michael Angelo. Admirers of Beethoven will use the argument that
the rugged grandeur of the Eroica Symphony,
and similar works, could not have flowed from
the pen of Mozart. Possibly not, but no more

could the sombre form of Beethoven be associated with the serene beauties of *Figaro* and *Don Giovanni.*

Godlike in self-abnegation, pure in life as the sacred themes which inspired the most perfect of his matchless melodies, the gentle spirit of Mozart drained to the bitter dregs the cup of misery which Genius ofttimes presents to the lips of her most favoured children.

Like some glorious star, lost in the mists and clouds of night to arise upon another world brighter, more radiant than before, so shines for us the light of his transcendent inspiration.

ROSSINI

1792-1868

FREQUENTERS of the Boulevards during the palmy days of the Empire little thought that the portly old gentleman who paraded his *embonpoint* day after day in the garb of a finished dandy, and who was bowed to obsequiously by scores of the *gommeux* of the day, had started life as a penniless peasant boy.

Yet such was the case. Gioachino Rossini was born in 1792. His father was an itinerant musician, and his mother was a second-class prima donna. His childhood was passed amid very modest surroundings. Travelling from town to town, and scraping together in coppers a precarious livelihood, the family often knew what it was to go to bed hungry. Soon matters grew worse; the father, an ardent patriot, allowed his zeal to get the better of his discretion, and, while he was suffering for his patriotic sentiments in prison, the boy and his mother

were entirely dependent on the gains of the
latter until they were rejoined by the husband.

It was very soon apparent that the child was
gifted with remarkable talent.   At an early age
he accompanied his parents on the piano, and
further contributed his share to the entertain-
ment by means of a good voice.   This accomplishment was not long lived; the voice weakened
and gradually disappeared altogether, and the
question then arose whether or not to have his
musical accomplishments perfected.   Tesei, who
was consulted, gave a favourable opinion, and
the lad was turned over to him, but he had
saddled himself with a troublesome pupil.
Most of Rossini's talent was derived from
inspiration ; long studies of counterpoint and
harmony did not commend themselves to his
lazy habits.   'You will never learn to compose
sacred music,' Tesei called out in despair,
'opera is all you will ever be good for!'   'And
quite sufficient!' was the saucy retort.

In 1810, when 18 years old, he composed his
first opera, *La Cambiale di Matrimonio*.   It had
only moderate success, but within the next two
years we come across eight operas written in
great haste and with the evident object to make
money.   None of these works point to the talent
of which the author stood possessed.   Had his

poverty not been absolutely galling, and, indeed, had Rossini been born in easy circumstances, it may well be doubted whether he would ever have astonished the world by his master-pieces; so little was his mind fired by any enthusiasm, or the sacred fire which generally works its way to the front when located in genius.

However, quite suddenly, unexpected by himself and without any special incentive, the opera *Tancredi*, composed for the Fenice, was so successful that the author leapt at one bound into the front rank of composers. The author himself acknowledges his indebtedness to Haydn and Mozart for the success achieved. The Italian school had deliberately ignored the great strides made by German composers. Melody was still their sole aim; the human voice pure and simple should reign in opera, and every admixture of harmony and orchestration was strictly eschewed as calculated to impair the importance of the singer. Rossini at once saw that this position could no longer be maintained. Had the daring revolution been inaugurated by an alien, the Italian public would probably have rejected it as a national insult; but Rossini, being one of their own countrymen, had the good luck to be not only forgiven but lauded to the sky for an innovation that had on the previous day been decried with scorn.

While still overwhelmed with the success of *Tancredi*, he scored an equal triumph with his next opera, *L'Italiana in Algieri*, but after that his compositions degenerated for a time in some inexplicable manner, and none of the operas turned out during the following years have been able to hold the boards.

In 1815 he followed Barbaja to Naples. This *impresario* knew how to treat the somewhat wayward composer. By plying him with good fare and drink, and pandering to a taste for luxurious habits which soon grew on the composer, he coaxed him into writing opera. Nevertheless he often found it a difficult task to overcome a constitutional laziness amounting to a disease. The *Barbiere di Siviglia*, written in three weeks, might have been delayed had not poverty acted as an incentive. Barbaja, at his wits' end, had stopped the supplies, and the composer, deprived of the means of buying firewood, had to write the score in bed. Rossini was a fervent admirer of *Figaro*; it was a favourite saying of his that Mozart's opera contained matter for twelve. He could not have taken a better model, nor could it have been more worthily followed. With the exception of

N

Figaro, the *Barbiere* is probably the most successful comic opera ever written.   Despite its great
merit, it was received on the first night with a
storm of derision ; popular antipathy manifested
itself in such an alarming degree that the composer, dreading a repetition, did not risk taking
his seat at the piano the next evening.   But the
reception on that occasion was totally different;
long and loud applause greeted the opera, and the
crowd that had only the day before execrated the
composer now deified him with wild adulation.

From that moment his financial status was
assured, and his name established for all future
time.   *Otello* and *La Gazza Ladra* wind further
wreaths around his brow, and when he arrives
at Vienna with his newly married wife, Isabella
Colbran, he is received with all the honours
of a recognised master.   At Vienna Rossini
appears   to   have   studied   German   music,
especially Mozart.   He had now the authority
needed to strike out boldly in a new direction,
and he had sufficient wisdom to discern how
far he could go without offending the ears of
his countrymen.   *Semiramide* burst upon the
world, and marks a further advance.   But while
conceding a wide field to harmony he was
careful to preserve the supremacy of melody,
without which no opera would hold the boards

in his country.   His undisputed genius enables
him to spice his works with refrains so sweet
and pleading that only Mozart's scores can be
said to excel them.

Still in the prime of youth, scarcely twenty-
three years of age, he severs his connection
with Barbaja and appears in London.   Here
as everywhere he is received with the greatest
distinction, and, when he arrives in Paris,
the offers made to him are so tempting that
he resolves to make that place his domicile.
The directorship of the Italian opera, one of
the most coveted prizes in the musical world, is
forced upon him.   It is a position of great
emoluments and equal responsibility, but, while
taking kindly to the first named condition, the
hard work is by no means suited to Rossini's
taste.   The opera languishes under its easy-
going director.   The authorities see that a
change is indispensable unless they wish to
ruin the institution.   At the same time the
government does not wish to offend Rossini.
A satisfactory solution is found.   The master,
elected Royal Superintendent of singing, retains
his salary, while the sinecure, which his title
virtually amounts to, enables him to pass his
days in the *otium cum dignitate* which is his
favourite condition.

Mosé in Egitto, composed in the twenty-seventh year of his age, is the next startling creation of his pen, given to the world after a long period of silence. It proves that in serious opera the composer is also qualified to hold his own. The prayer is among the finest music ever written, and stamps the master an efficient exponent of sacred music. Already the French style inaugurated by Auber asserts its influence, and some of the orchestral effects foreshadow the future course represented by the music of Meyerbeer. Again Rossini pauses for twelve years, satisfied to rest on his laurels as long as they are not seriously disputed. Then, roused by the phenomenal success of Auber's *Muette de Portici*, the old giant, if a man of thirty-nine may be called old, puts forward his best foot. This time his effort is well-planned, and, as he hopes, final. *Tell*, the greatest of all his masterpieces, is received from one end of Europe to the other with the most unqualified approval. It is rightly considered the great work of a great master. What might the world not expect from a composer, only thirty-nine years old, whose power stands in its very zenith? To what heights might this paragon not attain?

And now occurs one of the strangest phe-

nomena ever witnessed.   For thirty-seven long
years the master is silent, and during the whole
length of that time no opera and only one
piece of music worthy of his genius emanates
from his pen.   During that time other composers rise up around him.   Bellini, Donizetti,
Verdi, follow in his footsteps and carry his
principles to lengths that seriously compromise
the school he has inaugurated ; Meyerbeer
achieves successes beside which his own pale ;
Wagner lays the foundation of a new school
destined to attack all known principles ; and
yet the old lion sits still and makes no effort
to vindicate his right to a hearing.

The reason, though hard to believe, is not
difficult to find.   Happy in the possession of
ample riches, a lion of society, eagerly sought
and spoiled by the brightest gems of intellectual Paris, undisputed arbiter in the musical
world, his ambition is lulled to sleep.   Most
indolent of Epicureans, his life dream is fulfilled,
and while he can spread his huge form on
voluptuous couches he feels no incentive to put
to paper the ideas which, no doubt, were still
in profuse abundance beneath that bald cranium.
That restless fire which consumed the life-blood
of so many composers, whom death only could
tear away from their scores, was unknown to

the easy-going nature of Rossini.   Alternating
between his house in Paris, his villa in Passy,
and an occasional stay in Florence, Bologna,
Rome, he passed his days in luxurious comfort.

Only once did he emerge into the arena of
music.   It was to tender his last contribution,
the celebrated *Stabat Mater.*   The final *début*
was as brilliant as had been his earlier efforts.
As sacred music, the cantata has been pronounced too stagey in its melody and lacking
the solemn power of his own prayer in *Mosé*,
but from a musical point of view it is deservedly
characterised as a fine work.

The memory of Rossini is still comparatively
green.   It does not seem long ago since he
hobnobbed with many celebrities that may still
be met on the Boulevards.   As a reason for his
retirement from musical activity, his dissatis-
faction with political events has been more
than once alleged by people who were in a
position to know, and there may be some truth
in this assertion.   Rossini was nothing less
than a democrat.   The stiff-necked period of
the Restoration suited him best ; even Louis
Philippe was regarded by him in the light of a
socialist King, and the Republic of 1848 with
its Imperial development was not to his liking.
That a man of his obscure origin should have

gradually acquired the polish of a fine wit and thorough man of the world, renowned for rare conversational powers, is a great tribute to his versatility. But if he was renowned for puns and neatly worded repartee, he was also widely known for some astonishing crotchets. What, for instance, shall we think of a man who in the latter half of the nineteenth century refuses to enter a railway carriage and prefers travelling with post-horses, or who takes it into his head to farm all fisheries in Bologna ?

He was twice married. His first wife died in 1845, and in 1847 he married a lady of doubtful antecedents, with whom, however, he lived happily. Her beauty must have been considerable, as the celebrated Horace Vernet used to employ her as a model. Characteristic, too, is a remark that she made at the composer's death-bed : '*Moi, je resterai fidèle au nom de Rossini.*'

Rossini is unquestionably the foremost Italian composer of his age. None of his followers, Bellini, Donizetti, Verdi, have been able to reach, far less to eclipse, him. In many respects they have misinterpreted his teachings and rendered opera subservient to the ambition of singers to parade their capabilities. Bellini and Donizetti are the principal votaries of this

school, which finds its most determined anti-
thesis in the latest works of Wagner. In his
latest works Verdi appears to have evinced
leanings towards the teaching of the German
master, and the further development of Italian
opera will be watched with considerable interest.

SCHUBERT

1797-1828

NO more worthy shrine of pilgrimage exists for those in whom glows a spark of the sacred fire of music than the quiet unpretentious Währing cemetery of Vienna.

Here hidden among venerable trèes and old time-worn tombstones commemorating names long forgotten of this generation, we come first upon a plain marble slab inscribed with one word, but that word more eloquent in its solitude than the most magniloquent epitaph. It reads, 'Beethoven,' and three tombs further off a simple monument erected by loving hands to the memory of Franz Schubert. Its cost · is reported to have been less than twenty pounds ; but for a needy brother and a few friends not inexperienced in the bitter herb of hunger, this amount is the proof of noble sacrifice and ample devotion.

'This grave contains a rich treasure but still fairer hopes.' Alas ! the words are naught but truth. Thirty-one years old, another of that great immortal band whom a sorrowing world lost before it scarcely possessed them. Mozart, Schubert, Chopin, Weber, Shelley, Schiller, Byron, Keats—all entombed in the flower of their age—many of them without reaping the rewards of their glory.

Schubert was born at Vienna—the only one of the great composers that shed their light on the Kaiserstadt who was at the same time her son. His father followed the humble calling of a schoolmaster for a miserable stipend, which he must have often found difficult to reconcile with the fourteen children born to him. Franz displayed early capacity for music, and his first teacher, Holzer, soon avowed himself incapable of teaching him anything, and limited his functions to frequent expressions of astonishment. The next move was a scholarship in the Stadtconvict, a kind of preparatory school for the Imperial choristers, which was under the superintendence of Salieri and Eybler, then holding the principal official posts in the capital. The little lad in a grey suit, with his wild unruly shock of black hair and the spectacles which even at night were never off his nose, came in for considerable ridicule from the other boys seeking admittance, but the moment he raised his voice, the 'miller boy,' as they

mockingly called him, was appointed at once.
In the Stadtconvict, Schubert passed a number
of years. It was a gloomy establishment,
neither remarkable for a generous table nor for
a* great expenditure in fuel, and in winter the
poor boys clothed in the gold-braided Imperial
uniform had to huddle together and husband
their warmth and nourishment as best as they
could ; but in regard to music Schubert found
nothing to complain of. The noble works of
Haydn and Mozart meant more for him than a
plate of porridge. The inspired way in which
he went through his part could not fail to
impress the directors favourably. He was soon
promoted to the post of first violin, and when
the leader was indisposed he even took his part.
Even at this early age he composed sonatas,
masses, and songs. Spaun, an elder pupil, surprised him in this occupation, and expressed
his astonishment at this precocity. Schubert,
ever timid and bashful, had to be pressed for
some time before he pleaded guilty to composing,
adding that he could not repress his temptation
to do so, but that he was often unable to procure music-paper. In this respect and in many
others Spaun, who continued his friend to the
last, was of great service to him.

In 1810 he composed his first greater work :

a most gruesome corpse fantasy founded on
the doleful poem by Schiller ; this was written
as a duet for piano, but immediately afterwards
we come across two songs, *Hagar's Plaint* and
The Parricide, both of which show remarkable
talent.   In 1812 and 1813 quintetts, quartetts,
and even symphonies testify to the ambitious
nature of his tastes.   One and all are marked
by great independent ability, which every now
and then forces its way through the spirit of
Haydn and Mozart which still forms the under-
lying basis of his compositions.   The want of
contrapuntal knowledge, which is apparent
throughout his career, is pre-eminently so in
these first compositions, which show many of
the defects one would expect from an auto-
didact.

   In 1813, having just completed his sixteenth
year, Schubert bids adieu to the Stadtconvict
and takes up a post as assistant in his father's
school, an occupation for which he was little
fitted, and which could not remain permanent.
All the time he could spare was devoted to
composing and producing his music at the
Stadtconvict, with which institution he kept up
an unofficial connection.   In 1815 a vacancy
occurred at a great musical school in Laibach,
the disposal of which was mainly dependent

on the recommendation of Salieri. This much-honoured musical capacity, whose principal occupation would appear to have been the suppression of real genius, deserves a .passing notice in the history of music. Poor Mozart died under the impression that Salieri had poisoned him ; that accusation in a literal sense is no doubt unfounded, but that the death of Mozart and his utter misery must to a great extent be laid at the door of the Italian is not to be denied. We find him nevertheless in receipt of the greatest honours the Court has at its disposal, and virtually at the head of the musical circles at Vienna for over fifty years, during which Mozart, Haydn, Beethoven, Schubert, and Weber were his coevals. The only one to dislodge him in popular favour was Rossini, and this is a clear proof that Vienna as a resort of music was out of touch with the classical school that dwelt within its walls.

After this digression our readers will not be astonished to hear that Salieri favoured the claims of one Schaufl for the post at Laibach, while pretending all the time to Schubert's face that he was active on his behalf. Nevertheless they continued on friendly terms ; Salieri spoke of Schubert as a promising pupil, by which complimentary term he had also distinguished Beethoven ; and when somewhat later his own jubilee as Hofkapellmeister was celebrated with the greatest *éclat*, he did not hesitate to accept of a composition written in his honour by the composer he had tricked out of a position.

In 1815 and the following two years Schubert struck out in that direction by which his fame has become widest known. The music to Ossian's songs seems to have first led him to devote his attention to the writing of songs, so unique in style and excellence that, whatever we may think of him as an instrumental composer, his position as ' Lieder ' composer places him as *facile princeps* not only as regards the intrinsic value of the matchless gems traceable to his pen, but as originator of a school perpetuated by the more recent creations of Mendelssohn, Schumann, Brahms.

In judging of Schubert's ' Lieder ' we do not know which part to single out for special admiration. Is it the harmonious blending of text and melody, the appropriateness of every sentence, of every word, to the music set for it ? is it the flowing grace of the accompaniment unrivalled by any composer ? is it the thorough understanding of the poet's intention which led

Mayrhofer to say that he only understood his own poetry when he heard it set to music by his friend? is it the weird tone effects, the solemn and mysterious gliding from one key into another, which calls for greatest praise? We think that each question must be answered in the negative. We believe that Schubert's charm is the *tout ensemble*, the welding of all these considerations into one grand master-piece, the utter unsurpassable appropriateness of every particular of the most minute detail, which makes us say to ourselves—Thus and in no other way should this song have been written.

That a new field was opened up to Schubert, which he was the first to exploit, enhances the merit of his work, which in that particular branch had no previous works to lean on. The old lyric school, as distinguished from the romantic and new lyric schools of which Heine was the most pronounced type, had been brought to a rare state of perfection by Goethe and Schiller; its musical apotheosis was reserved to Schubert. Seventy-four of Goethe's and fifty-four of Schiller's poems he set to music in answer to Salieri's advice to avoid these two poets—advice that was quite typical of Salieri ; and judging by the correct interpretation of the sense of the poetry.

and the excellent taste displayed in the selec-
tion, people will be inclined to attribute to
Schubert literary tastes of the highest order.
Unfortunately this position cannot be upheld.
It is a remarkable fact that, besides gems of the
greatest value, his songs contain specimens of the
greatest literary trash imaginable. This applies
especially to his operas, which have invariably
been written to libretti so inferior that they are
in a great measure responsible for the fact that
they have not been produced.

As Schumann justly said, Schubert could
have written music for a placard. It is a most
astonishing phenomenon, this thirst for words
irrespectively of their value, and the capacity
to interpret everything into music invariably
appropriate and invariably beautiful.

Some of his most celebrated songs were
composed during those years following on 1815,
which were, at the same time, years of the greatest indigence and poverty, only to be compared
to the sad experiences of Mozart, who, however,
we must not forget, was burdened with a family.
At last temporary relief was afforded by an
engagement on the Hungarian estates of Count
Esterhazy. Here, in Zelesz, he finds a temporary haven, and during one happy summer he is
spared the pangs of hunger. Here also he

learns many Hungarian airs, traces of which are found in his later compositions. But the winter finds him back in Vienna composing, and alternating between fitful periods of sudden prosperity and just as sudden semi-starvation.

He was not to return to Zelesz for six years. The daughter of his host, Countess Caroline Esterhazy, had by that time matured into a young lady of the greatest beauty. Much has been written about an unfortunate love affair with her that-is said to have broken his heart, and there is an anecdote to the effect that he met her reproach at not having dedicated any of his compositions to her by the retort : ' Why should I ? everything I write is dedicated to you ! ' Unlike Beethoven, Schubert never seems to have been fascinated by women, and the distance socially between the composer and the Countess was too formidable ever to be bridged over, or ever to have rendered a love affair practicable.

All during this time, and, in fact, up to the composer's death, he was composing at post-haste. The most beautiful quartetts, the celebrated octett, the unrivalled symphonies, seem to have developed themselves under his pen with the power of magic, intersected by songs whenever and wherever a text presented itself.

O

The back of bills of fare, ragged bits of coarse
paper rudely lined, served on occasion as
receptacles for the most divine melodies.   But
Schubert never attached the importance they
deserved to his vocal compositions.   To be an
instrumental composer, and, beyond all, to be
a master in opera, was his principal dream.
In this latter respect he was never successful,
and unless the pains be taken to write appropriate words to his music, we fear he will never
be admitted into the circle of operatic composers.   The want of discrimination with which
he would set to work and compose a long opera
on the most impossible libretto would be ludi-
crous, were we not compelled to remember the
bitter disappointment which was no doubt
responsible for his early death.   Baraja, the
impresario who brought out Rossini, and who
subsequently owned two theatres at Vienna,
was cruel enough to alternately buoy up and
crush the hopes of the unfortunate man.   At
last the Musikakademie seemed to think well
of one of his works.   A rehearsal was granted,
and everything depended on the opinion of
Madame Schechner, the prima donna.   This
lady, by no means antagonistic to Schubert,
suggested a slight change in a passage that
tried her voice very much ; but he, though

nearly starving, would not alter a note of his
music, and on this obstinacy, which is perhaps
blamable, the whole matter suffered shipwreck.

Most touching was the reverential awe in
which he. held Beethoven, and this is to be
wondered at the more as his music, wherever
it is not strictly Schubert, has more in common
with Mozart. While he made no secret of his
personal leaning towards Beethoven, he often
regretted that his music should be far-fetched
and coupling together emotions that had nothing in common. For a long time he was
content to go to restaurants which the great
man frequented, and watch him from afar,
content to breathe the same air. At last,
however, greatly encouraged by Schindler. and
the publisher Diabelli, who probably thought
the approval of Beethoven would create a better
sale for Schubert's compositions, he resolved to
approach him in person. We can imagine the
trepidation in which Schubert, ever modest and
extremely bashful, approached the Olympian,
and tendered him the variations inscribed with
a most flattering dedication. Beethoven, in
one of his genial moods, handed him the paper
and pencil which, alas ! were his only means of
communication ; but the courage of Schubert,
never a very formidable quantity, had vanished,

and he stood trembling, not knowing what to write. Beethoven took the music and turned over the leaves until he came to one of the sins against counterpoint from which Schubert's best friends could not exonerate him. The scrupulous Beethoven good-humouredly pointed to the place in question, but that was too much for his visitor. Colouring to the roots of his hair, he beat a hasty retreat, and never stopped until he was in the next street and well out of the reach of his idol. Years afterwards, when the great master was on his deathbed, he pored over some of Schubert's songs ; he asked for more, and when he had looked through them attentively, he sent Schindler to fetch Schubert. 'That man has the divine fire ! I myself would have set these words to music if I had had them !' was the somewhat questionable compliment of the dying lion. When they saw one another it was already too late. What might the world not have seen if these two prodigies had suffered their genius to amalgamate, as did their literary coevals, Schiller and Goethe. In a few days Beethoven's remains were carried out to the Währing ceme-tery, Schubert following in the procession. On the way back he turned into a restaurant with two friends, and asked for two glasses of wine.

One he drank off to the memory of Beethoven, the other to that one of the three who should be the first to follow him. It proved to be himself.

The last year broke in when the bells tolled the new year of 1828. As if there had been foreknowledge, he worked with more feverish energy than ever. Some of his most sublime works, including his finest symphony and the touching songs comprised in the *Schwanengesang*—every word of which foretells death—must have added to the sadness overcast by physical distress and privation, which was never worse than in that year.

The death-hour came at three o'clock of the 19th November. He had only been ill for a short time; but of late it had occurred to him that the end was near, and he said as much to his brother Ferdinand, who sealed the affections of a lifetime by ministering to his last wants. At the last he was unconscious and delirious; but the name of Beethoven was ever on his lips, and his wish to be buried near him was religiously fulfilled. The inspiring strains of Mozart's Requiem which had been sung over Beethoven's ashes were also sung over Schubert's—a fitting tribute to the three immortal masters.

An inventory of Schubert's possessions enumerates a number of clothes and wearing apparel, and money to the value of sixty-three florins ; it includes ten florins for 'a lot of old music.' This must include over three-fourths of Schubert's total compositions—gems of the first order, unknown to humanity until long after his death.

It was reserved to Schumann to unearth these priceless possessions. As he was one of the few who knew and admired such of the few works of Schubert which had during his lifetime penetrated beyond a small circle, as he was among the small number of people to whom the death of the comparatively unknown man came as a severe shock—so it was only fitting that to him should be reserved the glory to procure for the *manes* of the divine master that worship which had been denied during a brief lifetime.

The name of Schubert soon became as celebrated as it had been obscure while he walked the earth. Mendelssohn, the all - important wielder of the bâton at the Leipzig Gewandhaus, brought his symphony in C into deserved prominence, and other instrumental pieces and Lieder were in the greatest request. Quite recently pieces have been rescued from oblivion, and there is no lack of devoted hands to carry on the search until all hope of adding to the list of his works is at an end.

Characteristic is a notice in a Paris paper which appeared in 1839. Referring to the great number of posthumous works that were constantly being brought forward under the authorship of Schubert, it pointed to the evident abuse of this name, as it appeared quite impossible that this composer should have left so many works unpublished. The argument is pardonable ; at that time the life of Schubert was wrapped in obscurity, and few people were aware of the sad circumstances which rendered by far the greater portion of his works posthumous.

Curiously enough, the British public, generally laudably docile in the matter of music, refused at first positively to listen to Schubert's music. ' A vastly over-rated man,' ' no music,' ' wild trash,' were some of the arguments used freely. This injustice has been long condoned, and at the present time some of his most fervent admirers dwell in 'the foggy island !

In appearance Schubert was insignificant ; his height, scarcely over five feet, was further encroached upon by a continual stoop, round shoulders, fat arms, and stumpy fingers ; his

features were broad and unimposing ; his hair,
wild and shaggy, environed a pasty pale com-
plexion; but the eyes were very fine and seemed
to penetrate the glasses which he always wore,
and they alone bear outward witness to his
sublime soul.

In language and inclinations he was essentially Viennese : gay and good-humoured and
generous to excess.   Unlike Beethoven, whose
rugged nature exacted the homage even of
those whom it offended, Schubert was retired
and self-effacing.   Instead of making friends
in the better circles, he surrounded himself
with a number of good-hearted but moneyless
young men who could not appreciate him
according to his merits, and, unaware of his
own needy circumstances, which he disguised
as much as possible, lived on his pocket and
drained his resources.   To a great extent his
poverty was due to improvidence.   While
money was procurable he literally threw it
away, and never stopped until the last copper
was gone.   Then he set about to procure more ;
and publishers, who seem to have been in all
ages remarkably good business men, traded on
his needs and doled out their money in a very
cautious way, and against a fair equivalent in
brain-work.   Thus many of his immortal songs
changed ownership at 10½d.

Perhaps this absence of the sense of ' manage-
ment,' which is such a constant concomitant of
musical genius, points to the fact that the
essentially inward direction which the thoughts
of musicians must take is incompatible with the
exigencies of the outer world, simple though
they may seem to us more worldly individuals.

SCHUMANN

1810-1856

THERE is an inexorable law which applies to all matters within the range of our understanding, and from which no institution, social or political, no branch of art and no field of human action is exempt. It decrees that every period of abnormal activity should be followed by one of lassitude and inactivity, and that the depression thereby caused becomes stagnant in proportion to the activity of the preceding era of reform and upheaval.

The lustrum closing with the death of Beethoven and Schubert had been like none other productive of giants in the musical world. Commencing with Bach and Handel, it had gradually produced Gluck, Haydn, Mozart, Beethoven, Schubert, following on one another in such rapid succession that the less perceptive capacities of the music-loving public may be well excused for desiring an age of comparative repose after one of incomparable excitement.

The last great men of the preceding generation had been hardly carried to their graves when a reaction, as decisive and irresistible as had been the storm which swept away the old prejudices, declared itself. For years the classical masters were consigned to oblivion. A small and select band of adherents, indeed, never relaxed in their allegiance and kept the lamp of incense aflame, but the general public clamoured for simple melody combined with the meretricious effect of empty fireworks requiring executive skill without the fire of genius. A school of pianists sprang up in obedience to the public call, and performed before admiring audiences a plethora of operatic airs, never meant for their instrument, hidden by variations and brilliant accompaniments, well executed, but calculated rather to show the individual accomplishment of the player than the intrinsic value of the piece. Scores of composers, or rather adapters, of this class of music rose up and took possession of the public fancy, as if no music had been written for the pianoforte, and lovers of this instrument were compelled to borrow music from operatic scores, and thus declare their incapacity to appreciate original creations.

Two men arose to combat this unnatural development. They succeeded, by works of their own, in leading back the public taste into healthier grooves and in restoring to their legitimate position the old classical masters on whose teachings their own works were largely based, and of whom they were worthy followers. These two men, whose influence is still in the ascendant, are Mendelssohn and Schumann. We have already seen how the former purified the romantic school and paved the way for his younger contemporary, who, incomparably more vigorous, more daring, and more radical— not content to reform existing abuses, but braving public opinion in the face of continued disapproval—struck out a path eminently different from anything hitherto seen, and destined to be appreciated only after the untimely demise of its originator.

Schumann was born at Zwickau of well-to-do parents. At a very early age he showed musical talents, which were encouraged to a degree, although both father and mother, but especially the latter, did not wish their son to adopt music as a vocation. When the father died, in 1820, Robert gave up for the nonce all hopes to make his inclinations prevail over the determination of the mother. He was intended for a legal career, and for this purpose entered the Leipzig University in 1828, when eighteen years old. A worse place to damp his musical ardour could not well have been chosen. Leipzig had just been raised by the genius of Mendelssohn to the foremost rank in musical Germany. The celebrated Gewand-haus concerts, presided over by the bâton of that master, exercised a supremacy which was felt far beyond the confines of Saxony, and the atmosphere was so heavily laden with music of the best kind that enthusiasm was kindled in the souls of musicians far less inspired than the excitable Schumann. To say that his legal studies were neglected would be a very mild term indeed ; we have it on his own admission that when he left the next year for Heidelberg he had made considerable progress in piano-forte practice, but that as regards law his mind was a blank. In Heidelberg things were not much better. From time to time he seems to have felt some remorse at the neglect of his duties ; this led to his taking a *refectorium*, by which is meant a course of repetition to acquire the knowledge he had so far neglected to acquire; but the attempt ended in a failure, and he came to the conclusion that he would never qualify for the law. The opposition of the mother, when approached on the subject, was as strong as might be expected. To discard all dreams of ambition culminating in a government appointment for her son, and to see this hope of her declining age 'deteriorate' into a musician, was a hard nut for the obstinate old lady.   But Robert, though not the most determined of beings, and as a rule easily swayed, was equally firm.   He was now twenty years of age, and could ill afford to waste further time if he wanted to follow the profession of his choice. At last he prevailed, and settled down to a course of study at Leipzig under Wieck, his future father-in-law.

For a long time he doubted his capacity to become a composer, and perhaps it was only to an accident that the repertory of music owes some of its brightest gems.   This accident—a source of great regret at the time—consisted in nothing less than a strain to the third finger of the right hand, brought about by incessant playing.   Though partially healed later on, this settled at once all possibility of his becoming a soloist.   He had written several small pieces, regarding the value of which he felt by no means sanguine; but, now driven to his pen, he put all his energy into the composition of a symphony which he fondly hoped would meet with success.   The first part had already been performed at Zwickau, young Clara Wieck, at that time a girl of thirteen, taking the solo part, and, as Schumann aptly said, 'firing Zwickau for the first time in its existence with enthusiasm;' but a performance of the entire symphony resulted in something very like a failure, and the work has never been printed.

This repulse was no doubt the cause of his decision to embark in musical journalism. The *Neue Zeitschrift*, started with a few friends, soon took a commanding position among its compeers. The age, too, was ripe for criticism of a searching nature; few papers existed, and among those none were sufficiently independent to break with the powers of the day. The attack upon prevailing abuses with a pen both able and impartial has been one of the principal merits of Schumann. As a writer, his works take a high degree, and as a critic he deserves the rare praise of combining fearless exposure of charlatanism with frank appreciation of real worth.

Schumann was nothing if not mystical. His leaning towards Jean Paul, the archetype of that exaggerated school of emotion, apt to become morbid in its intensity, for which the German mind seems to be more receptive than less metaphysical nationalities, characterises the man. 'Jean Paul has often brought me to the verge of desperation,' was one of his frequent sayings, and yet he remained constant to his ideal until his reason became obscured, partly, perhaps, through the gloomy teachings of an occult symbolism. Taking this circumstance into account, it is surprising that a brisk wave of freshness proceeds not only from his terse and vigorous pen, but also from his music, which often alternates in crisp sharpness and dreamy mysticism. But one element at least bears witness to the influence of Jean Paul, and is of frequent recurrence, not only in the broadsheets of his paper, but in the music which at that period was given to the world. We refer to the mysterious introduction of Florestan, Eusebius, and the Davidsbündlers, which traverse his whole activity like marionettes paraded across the stage. With regard to the two former denominations, they were doubtless meant to represent two tendencies in his own individuality, and are introduced as arguing against one another, while the Davidsbündler is a mysterious supposed combination of the real talent fighting against the Goliath of stupidity and pedantry.

But while hard at work on this paper, Schumann was composing vigorously all the time, and a number of his best compositions are found among these first productions of his pen. It is noticeable that the critics were from the outset favourable to his style, while the public failed to comprehend forms so revolutionary and melodies so fantastically wild and original.

In 1835 Mendelssohn arrived at Leipzig, and a devoted friendship springs up almost immediately between the two men. While Schumann, however, idealised the elder master and looked up to him as one far beyond what he could ever aspire to, Mendelssohn did not at first appreciate Schumann as a composer, though afterwards he was the first to confess his mistake.

In 1837 the mutual love which united him to Clara Wieck reached a climax. He proposed, but the father, possibly having higher aspirations for the gifted girl, refused, alleging the uncertain position of Schumann. To satisfy this demand he determined to transfer his paper to Vienna, hoping to find a good field in that city, which still preserved its musical halo. The result was not encouraging, and so many difficulties were placed in his way that, in 1839, he returned to Leipzig and renewed his suit for Clara's hand. Again the father objected, and forced the lovers to invoke the decision of the law, which pronounced in favour of the marriage.

Though sorely tried by these obstacles, which

P

had a most distressing effect on the susceptible mind of the composer, he found a sweet recompense in the era of unmixed happiness which followed on his marriage. His activity redoubled, and some of his most inspired songs, some of his finest pieces for piano and orchestra, were written under the stimulating influence of a happy love, which until his death united those two gifted beings.

In 1841 he made a second trip to Vienna, where he composed the *Faschingsschwank*. As a protest against the official obstruction he had met with in this city he inserted in this piece several bars of the Marseillaise, an air strictly prohibited by the anti-revolutionary government. On visiting Beethoven's grave he found a steel pen on the tombstone, which he appropriated. We can imagine the importance a man of his impressionable nature would attach to such an incident. The pen was treasured up as never had been steel pen before ; only on the most important occasions was it uesd. His own symphony in E and the enthusiastic report on Schubert's C major symphony were among the few privileged writings to which it was to give effect.

In 1844 he left Leipzig for Dresden. A mental affection, which was to ripen into insanity later on, had been brought on by over-work, and the doctors insisted on his leaving the music-loving town. Schumann had always been of a silent disposition, but at times his apathy became so alarming that his friends were most anxious. In his favourite restaurant he would sit for hours turning his back to the company and humming melodies without heed to questions addressed to him. Later on matters became worse; a fixed idea gained hold on him that he was always hearing one note or one harmony, and gradually his intercourse with his family would be saddened by that grave, uncanny, silence.

For a long time he lived in Dresden incapable of work, limiting his activity to the leadership of a choral union, until at 1849 he felt quite recovered from his disease, having remained for five years as if obscured from the world of music. His last appointment as Kapellmeister at Düsseldorf was unsuccessful. Schumann was not fitted for that post; in fact it is difficult to imagine a composer of his rank who was a worse conductor. His works met with great success and were rapturously applauded in the Rhenish city, but the authorities arrived at the conclusion, which might have been postponed but never obviated, that they could not retain the master in his position. We cannot say whether this decision might

have been communicated in a way less calculated to hurt the feelings of one so sensitive,
but as a fact it may have contributed largely
to intensify the gloom which was already
spreading over his diseased imagination. The
last years of his life were unconsciously approaching. Voyages to Switzerland and Holland were productive of some short spells of
satisfaction, and a cool reception at Leipzig did
not produce the evil effects his friends dreaded ;
but in reality he was fast declining, and his
apathy was due to a general breaking up of the
whole system.

All his worst eccentricities were in full bloom
since 1852. His wife and daughters, unable to
alleviate his mental sufferings, were compelled
to look on inactively while this splendid genius
was going to rack and ruin. There were indeed
some lucid intervals, but these only sufficed to
accentuate the contrasting periods of desponding
absence of mind which increased in frequency
and intensity as time went on.

. Once more Schumann took up the pen for
his newspaper after a silence extended over
years. The article was entitled ' Neue Bahnen '
(new paths), and hailed the advent of a new
musical Messiah in the person of Brahms, who,
the master said, had come into the world in

the full maturity of a composer worthy to be styled the successor of Beethoven. Many were the tongues at the time who characterised this praise as fulsome and not warranted by facts. But the world is now .alive to the value of Brahms, and gives Schumann credit for his perspicacity and sound judgment.

On the 27th February 1854, without previous warning, Schumann quitted his house and jumped into the Rhine, and, though rescued by some boatmen, the shock had been too violent; insanity declared itself, and he had to be taken to an asylum near Bonn, in which, with occasional lucid intervals, he passed the remainder of his days. On the 29th of July 1856 he breathed his last in the arms of his devoted wife, whose love had never failed him. Though death had been imminent since his melancholy had induced him to seek a watery grave, the news came as a severe shock on the musical world, which could not be insensible to the immense services the dead master had rendered to his art. The worship of Schumann, only partial during his lifetime, is still increasing. Of all composers he is the most strikingly original, and his excellence has been proved in every branch of the art which he has essayed.

As oratorio, *Paradise and the Peri* ranks with

the best productions of all ages ; his own opera
Genoveva bids fair to secure a lasting place
on the German stage ; his symphonies and
orchestrated pieces are the best since Beethoven,
and for the piano, the only instrument he could
play, he has opened up a delightful variety of
possibilities, ranking from the height of gaiety
to the depth of emotional feeling. A special
word remains to be said about his songs. He
is a fitting cornerstone in the triumvirate of
which the other two participants are Mendelssohn and Schubert. The latter is perhaps his
superior in melody and the former in finish, but
Schumann leaves the other two behind him in
depth of emotion and vigour.

In fact we think a comprehensive digest of
his music would establish his pre-eminence
over many of his compeers in the matter of
vigour and emotion, two qualities very different and rarely found together, but in him
happily blended in a state of ideal perfection.

And of these same qualities Schumann was
a physical representative. Full and strongly
built, with square massive features, broad jaw
and firm-set mouth, his frame seemed cast in
iron. Unluckily it was set off by a highly
nervous and irritable temperament, a tendency
towards melancholy, and a sensitiveness to

opposition and disagreeable matters which amounted to an anguish nearly mortal and a helplessness rare of its kind.

Let us add that his nature was of the noblest. No particle of that envy which is frequently inherent even in artistic greatness can be traced to his pen. His criticisms on all contemporary musicians are models of clear conciseness, and show ample appreciation even where it was not returned.

WAGNER

1813-1883

THERE are those who believe in an un-written law, according to which genius, however oppressed, however obscured it may be by surrounding circumstances, must, like the rays of the sun, eventually penetrate the densest of clouds and wax victorious above its late enemies. These people allow no credit to adventitious circumstances, none to the timely appearance on the battle-field of a *deus ex machinâ*, without whose generous aid it is difficult to see how genius could have procured that crust of bread which even the most gifted of mankind cannot dispense with.

As a true knight militant of his vocation, a hero of energy, a fighter whom defeat could only render more obstinate, Wagner cannot be easily matched, and yet it is hard to imagine that his name would have emerged from the heap of obloquy, ridicule, and censure which buried it out of sight, had not a mighty friend arisen for him, a man comparable only to his

232

own impersonations of Lohengrin and Tannhäuser. A figure of mediæval chivalry, eccen-
tricity, romance, a veritable Don Quixote—
perhaps the only one that has existed in our
days—that belated Minstrel-King came into
the world seven hundred years behind his time,
and was placed by a satirical freak of nature on
a throne of the realistic, practical, business-like,
anti-sentimental wane of the nineteenth century.

Poor, generous, poetic Ludwig of Bavaria!
You were not born to review battalions, to
receive frock-coated ambassadors, to have
your actions bespattered by the venom of *fin
de siècle* papers; your place was among the
Minnesingers of old, the warriors of the lyre,
the bidders for the grace of 'ladye faire,' the
knightly order of the Holy Graal. He knew it
well; there was self-conscious significance in
those princely edifices which arose like magic
on lofty crags, inaccessible save to a trusted
few, secluded from the vulgar gaze, where, at
the witching hour of night, the royal hermit
would disport himself on lonely lakes, clad in
the long forgotten garb of a mythical age. He
knew it well when in the limpid mountain lake
he sought a watery grave rather than give up
his enchanting dream, true to the last to romance, true to the last to his rôle as troubadour,

that idealistic fiction to which the vitiated air of our world would be as subtle poison.

Was Ludwig mad ?   There are many still who think otherwise.   But whether mad as a man and as a sovereign, as an artist he was sublime, and by the world of music his name will ever be revered as the preserver of Wagner !

For now at last it is acknowledged on all hands that the preservation of Wagner is a meritorious act.   The fight against him has been long and bitter.   In its intensity nothing can be found to equal it.   Rival factions have intensified their strife with all the venom of spiteful animosity.   'There is no one to approach the master' is the cry of his adherents, proudly dubbing with this exclusive title the object of their affection.   'Wagner is nothing but a charlatan, totally devoid of genius, totally devoid even of the sense of music' is retorted by assailants every whit as fierce.   Even an authority usually calm and impartial, the weighty and judicial Fétis, pronounces in 1864 that Wagnerism is dead and buried, and that the operas of *Tannhäuser* and *Lohengrin* are already forgotten.   We in 1892 know better than that.   Whatever may be the fate of the master's later works—and in regard to them

the smoke of the battle has not yet cleared—
we know that few operas are more popular than
the ones known.   We know also that even
Paris, unbelieving Paris, prejudiced against
Wagner as a German among Germans, after
first making the performance of his music a
subject of political dissension, now listens with
rapture to the strains, and unequivocally admits
their overwhelming merit.

To decry the productions of a composer who
has worked his way to the front in the teeth of
universal opposition, as senseless trash, is
ridiculous; on the other hand, those who
elevate Wagner to the situation of first of all
the great are probably equally wide of the
mark.   Because Wagner is a great musician
there is no need for Bach, Mozart, Beethoven,
and others to abdicate.   Because he is a radical
reformer, it does not follow that the whole
school of opera will follow in his wake; indeed,
there are serious reasons against it, reasons of
cost, reasons of time, and finally, reasons of
popular taste.   Yet, had he done nothing
beyond giving to us *Lohengrin* and *Tannhäuser*,
the name of Wagner would shine as a star of
the first order in the musical firmament.

Many are coming round to that opinion.
'He possesses genius,' they say; 'the pity is

that it is employed in the wrong cause.' But is there not something like divine inspiration required to produce that dogged determination, that invincible fixity of purpose, that fierce obstinacy, only intensified by maddening reverses and the bitter condiment of pecuniary adversity, for which his equal cannot be found? Ought the work of a man to be condemned beforehand—who, hunted down by creditors, belittled by critics, hooted out of theatres, and pursued by that most galling of scourges, ridicule, sits down to compose that trilogy? This, the most attacked of all his works, is a giant conception, which, as he sadly writes, he knows he can never hope to hear during his life-time, a work which necessitates a special theatre and other expenses, before which even the admirers of his most successful competitor, Meyerbeer, might have stood aghast, while he, ill-starred enthusiast, cannot obtain a hearing for his less pretentious works.

The master has been so recently among us, his name and exploits have been so much a matter of our own generation, that we find it difficult to realise that he was only a few years younger than Mendelssohn, Schumann, Chopin, all of whom long dead, appear to us in the light of history far removed. Born at Leipzig in

1813, he inherited theatrical and literary tastes from his father, who was fond of disporting himself on the amateur stage. Several of his brothers and sisters adopted the stage as a profession, and at least two of them attained to a high degree of excellence. To complete the character of these surroundings, his step-father, Geyer, of whom Wagner always spoke with the greatest affection, was also an actor. It does not appear that the boy, though otherwise exceptionally gifted, had a talent for painting; and yet this was the vocation which for a short time was selected for him. At school, in Dresden, whither the family soon emigrated, his progress in classics, and especially in German composition, was so remarkable that it was thought he would become a poet. And here it may be remarked that the literary abilities of Wagner are somewhat unjustly overshadowed by his more brilliant achievements as a musician. Yet these are so considerable that, had he elected literature as a calling, he would no doubt have made a mark. As it is, some of his extant writings show considerable merit.

There are the usual traces of immature, early work. A grand tragedy has been preserved from his fourteenth year; it contains forty-two deaths, and, as he laughingly said, some of the dead had to come back as ghosts in the fifth act to keep it going. But a removal from Dresden to Leipzig, in consequence of the death of Geyer, led to an entire change in his vocation. The performance of Beethoven's symphonies at the Gewandhaus drove him irresistibly into the path of music. He had always been partial to Weber's compositions, but it had never before occurred to him that music should become the absolute mistress of his soul. He now borrowed a work on 'thorough bass,' and commenced to study in order to write the music for his own tragedy. Luckily this remained in embryo; another overture proved to him that he was anyhow not yet a Beethoven. The drum had to give a tap fortissimo every four bars, and the public grew fairly bewildered and considered it a joke. 'This was the height of my absurdities,' Wagner remarks in his autobiography, and we can well believe it.

Soon, however, he received able tuition from Weinlig, whose methodical knowledge proved of the greatest value. He studied very hard and acquainted himself thoroughly with all the greater works of Beethoven, most of which he copied out in score. In 1832 he wrote a symphony framed on Beethoven and Mozart's

music. With this work he hoped to take
Vienna by storm, but he found that capital so
absorbed by Hérold's *Zampa* and Strauss's
waltzes that he returned immediately. It was
afterwards submitted to Mendelssohn, but the
matter quite escaped his memory, and the
young composer was too proud to remind him.
At Prague in 1832 he wrote his first libretto,
Die Hochzeit, but money was becoming scarce,
and he was only too glad to obtain an appointment at Würzburg as chorus-master at the
beggarly salary of 10 florins per month. Back
in Leipzig in 1834, he saw for the first time
the celebrated singer Wilhelmine Schröder-
Devrient, whose magnificent acting and singing
had a commanding influence on him. For
several years he was associated with her in
Dresden in daily communication. When composing or writing she was in his mind's eye
whenever he conceived a new character, and
there is no doubt that her imposing talent
induced in him that craving after the closest
possible combination of acting and music which
he carried to the greatest known extreme.

At Magdeburg, where his footsteps next led
him, an attempt was made to produce his first
opera, *Das Liebersverbot*, founded on Shake-
speare's *Measure for Measure* ; but so little time

was allotted to the rehearsals that the performance resulted in a perfect chaos.

Unsuccessful attempts to stage the opera in
Leipzig and Berlin, and increasing pecuniary
troubles, drove the composer to take up a
situation at Königsberg, and thence, after the
director had become bankrupt, at Riga, where
he was enabled to make sufficient money to
pay off his most pressing debts. At Königsberg he married his first wife, Miss Planer,
whom he had met at the theatre. But the
Eldorado for operatic composers of that day
was Paris. The enormous profits made by
Meyerbeer could not fail to dazzle the eyes of
musicians with whom life at the best was a
kind of semi-starvation. Sketches of an opera,
Die hohe Braut, were sent to the all-powerful
Scribe, but of course an obscure composer writing from a provincial town on the Baltic was
not deemed worthy of an answer. At Riga
the novel *Rienzi*, by Bulwer, suggested the opera
of that name; Wagner worked hard at the
libretto, determined to try his luck with this
opera personally in Paris.

At last he left in 1839 by ship *via* London,
accompanied by his wife and a large Newfound-
land dog. The voyage was memorable and full
of dangerous incident. For three weeks the

passengers were tossed about, and the angry waves suggested ideas in him which afterwards took shape in the *Flying Dutchman*. At Boulogne he made the acquaintance of Meyerbeer, to whom he was recommended. Whether Wagner was indebted to Meyerbeer for introductions which came to nothing, or whether, as has been suggested, the latter designedly refrained from helping him in the right quarter, will probably never be known. Impartial judges, among whom Heine is best known, have expressed sarcastic doubts as to Meyerbeer's disinterestedness. On the other hand, Wagner has been profusely blamed for the very vigorous onslaught he made in the press on the maestro's music. That Wagner honestly disagreed with the tendency of the composer of the *Huguenots* cannot be doubted, and that a critic as such should not be swayed by reasons of personal gratitude, supposing them to exist, stands to reason.

The three years, 1839-42, passed in Paris are among the most miserable of his life. Everything seemed to go wrong with the irritable man, whose idiosyncrasies were diametrically opposed to the French world he was living in. Even Liszt, his most devoted apostle of later years, came in for the biting satire of his pen.

His only friends were among the crowd of warm-hearted but poor German artists and Bohemians who swarmed in Paris. 'Were it not for many friends,' he wrote, 'I and my little wife would starve.' It is worth noting that some literary trifles, favourably commented on, served to add a meagre trifle towards his very meagre income. The *Flying Dutchman*, written in the days of his greatest adversity, pleased Pillet, the director of the Variétés so much that he proposed to buy the libretto and entrust it to another composer. We need hardly mention that Wagner rejected this proposal with great scorn. Before leaving Paris he commenced the libretto of *Tannhäuser*, which struck him at once as a suitable legend whereon to construct a popular opera. He did not however undertake this task without a preliminary course of severe historical study, which also led to the elaboration of the plot of his later opera, *Lohengrin*. In the midst of this work the unwelcome news arrived from Leipzig and Munich that the *Dutchman* had been rejected as unsuitable for the German stage. 'I had hoped it would touch chords that respond quickest with Germans!' were his sad words on receipt of this news.

When matters were at the lowest ebb a stroke of fortune came to the composer which

bade fair to place him beyond want for the
remainder of his days.   Not only was he
appointed Kapellmeister at Dresden, but the
complete success of his opera *Rienzi* placed his
name on a pinnacle which only a short time
before had seemed quite beyond his reach.
The excitement in the musical world must
have been remarkable.   Wagner was spoken of
as the new musical Messiah ; so great was the
enthusiasm that Tichatschek, the celebrated
tenor, refused point blank to have a trifling
excision made from his part.   The *Flying
Dutchman* was now vociferously demanded, but
to the general surprise of the public it fell flat.
The composer, greatly mortified, was consoled
by a letter from Spohr, who alone of his great
contemporaries wrote of the opera in terms of
unstinted praise.   It was well for Wagner's
pecuniary prospects that the success of *Rienzi*
outbalanced this comparative failure ; had it
been otherwise, the confirmation of his post as
Kapellmeister might have been withheld.   As
it is, he seems to have accepted the post with
some misgivings.   His republican nature chafed
at royal protection ; art, he rightly argued,
ought to be independent ; in the end, however,
more sage counsels prevailed, and the seven
years of comparative quietude which now

followed must have compared to advantage with the *Künstlers Erdenwallen* of Königsberg and Paris.

Tannhäuser soon absorbed him so entirely that not only was the failure of the *Dutchman* for the time forgotten, but also his resolution to seek the approval of the few and not appeal again to the fickle favours of the hydra-headed crowd. *Tannhäuser* he thought would do what the previous opera had failed in : it would electrify the masses and be a repetition on a larger scale of the success of *Rienzi*. But, strange to say, the first performances bewildered not only the audience but the singers. 'You are a man of genius,' said his friend, Madame Schröder-Devrient, 'but you write such eccentric stuff it is hardly possible to sing it.' The critics took up the refrain, and for a time the vain and self-opinionated master was the best abused man in the musical world. ' No melody,' ' distressing, harassing music,' ' nerve killing,' are some of the judgments scattered broadcast by writers who thus took revenge for many personal slights they may have experienced in their personal intercourse. The master, much chagrined, responded in a characteristic way by commencing forthwith on *Lohengrin*. Not for a moment did he doubt the public was at fault; theirs was the blame and theirs the misfortune if they could not appreciate his music. Mendelssohn is so faint in his praise that it amounts to censure, Spohr qualifies his approval, but Schumann is more appreciative. Liszt was the first to reproduce the opera at Weimar, and other cities followed at long intervals. Berlin refused for a long time to place the opera on the boards, and the King, who was approached on the subject, made the characteristic proposal that some of the music should be set to military instruments so that he might form an idea of its value. It is needless to describe Wagner's feelings on receiving this proposal.

In 1848 the instrumentation of *Lohengrin* was finished, and the master was already sketching out the plan of the trilogy which was destined to become his most important work. Revolutionary troubles soon absorbed the mind of the public. Though Wagner's sympathies were undoubtedly on the popular side, the position he took up does not appear to have been otherwise than moderate, and certainly not sufficiently aggressive to warrant the severe measures of which he was soon to be made the subject. His principal sin seems to have been the expression of a hope

that political reforms would lead to a better
state of things in musical and theatrical matters.
The premature plan of a 'national theatre' was
ample reason to stamp him a dangerous
character, and he was none too soon in putting
the French boundary between himself and the
Saxon police.

There commenced now a period of twelve
years, 1849-1861, during which Wagner was
expatriated from the country of his birth.
After a short stay in Paris he settled down in
Zürich, the favourite dwelling-place of many
German refugees.   With no immediate prospect
of earning a living by his art, he launched into
a feverish literary activity.   His works principally touched on the state of music ; they
contain a complete exposé of his artistic aims,
and form a commentary on his compositions
which is of the greatest value to the student of
their history and meaning.   From this time
dates the pamphlet, *Hebraism in its Relation to
Music*, which has made much noise, and cannot
perhaps be defended from all points of view,
though it was not intended as an indictment
against the Jewish race, but rather as a protest
against those composers and critics who, at that
time, were most antagonistic to him, and who,
headed by Meyerbeer, happened to belong to

the Jewish faith. No doubt Wagner, never quite just, and at that moment smarting under the most cruel reverses, chiefly undeserved, was less than ever disposed to bridle his tongue when contrasting his position as an exile with the princely honours rendered to Meyerbeer.

But though absent from Germany, his final recognition in that country as a master of music was soon to come. On 28th August 1850, Liszt produced *Lohengrin* at Weimar. The success was enormous. A large concourse of musical and literary authorities had been gathered together, and the sacred date of Goethe's birth gave additional lustre to a phenomenal performance. From this date, though the income of the composer remained problematical, his fame among a large section of German musical opinion was firmly established.

The next years passed without much incident. A trip to London, and a memorable connection with the Philharmonic Society, is still green in the memory of English contemporaries. But in the intervals Wagner was hard at work. *Siegfried*, *Rheingold*, *Walküre* take shape in his active brain, and already the plans for *Tristan and Isolde*, and *Parsifal*, are nearly matured. In 1857 he resolved to devote all his energies to *Tristan*. For one brief moment a fit of discouragement seized him. Why continue this hopeless work on the *Nibelungen*? Would it ever be performed, and, anyhow, could he ever live to see it? In 1859 *Tristan* was finished, but to get it performed was one of the greatest difficulties Wagner ever had to contend with. The King of Saxony was inexorable; even the personal intercession of several German princes could not procure his permission to return to Dresden, and negotiations to produce the opera elsewhere led to nothing.

Heartbroken, the composer went to Paris, bent on the apparently hopeless task of getting *Tannhäuser* performed. The difficulties seemed so insurmountable that he had already made up his mind to return to Switzerland, when the influence of the Countess Metternich with the Emperor broke down all barriers. The greatest preparations were made, celebrated singers engaged, and no expense spared, but the cabal of Wagner's enemies was too powerful, and the performance resulted in the most serious defeat he had ever experienced. After three performances, to an audience turbulent in their discontent, the attempt to force *Tannhäuser* on the Paris public had to be abandoned, the

Opera Company having spent over £8000 to no purpose.

Now at last the interdict banishing Wagner from Germany was removed; he re-entered that country in 1861, and was everywhere well received, the bad treatment he had experienced in Paris being a point in his favour. Everywhere his operas were performed to enthusiastic houses, but it was due to the peculiar copyright laws of Germany that he reaped next to nothing from this success, and his pecuniary position had seldom been worse than during the three years now ensuing.

Then at last came the turning-point in his life. The young King Ludwig II. of Bavaria, who had just succeeded to his father's throne, sent for Wagner and offered him a stipend out of his private purse. From this time onward life passed for the composer as a beautiful dream, hard to realise after the ample share of hardships and misfortunes that had fallen to his lot. Enemies still emptied the vials of their wrath over him; even at Munich the cabal was so strong that he had to give up his residence there, but the favour of the King triumphed over all difficulties, and to the end his gracious patronage was never withdrawn from his most celebrated subject. The

Meistersinger, commenced 1846, was rapidly
completed and performed at Munich in 1868.
Now that care no longer dictated his movements,
the *Nibelungen* were rapidly drawing towards
their completion.   In 1870 the score was in
the printer's hands, and in August of that
year, while Germany was in the midst of her
victorious career in France, he married his
second wife, Cosima von Bülow, the daughter
of his tried friend Liszt.

Wagner societies were now formed all over
Germany.   Money flowed in from all sides.
Even from abroad considerable sums found
their way to the central office.   Places so
widely distant from one another, both as regards space and sympathies, as St. Petersburg,
Paris, Warsaw, New York, Amsterdam, Cairo,
Stockholm, London, vied with the composer's
own country in finding the funds towards that
architectural dream which soon became reality
in the little town of Bayreuth.   Unable in the
prime of his life to obtain a hearing on any
condition, the master ended by imposing his
own ideas on followers only too glad to obey
blindly the most unusual dictates of his
fancy.

With regard to his later music, which in and
after 1876 has drawn thousands to the quiet

Franconian town, opinions vary pro and contra.
'No melody' is the war-cry of opponents, but
then the same had been the original verdict
of people who now wax enthusiastic over
Tannhäuser. The advent of Wagner is too
recent to admit of a calm judgment. In later
years, when the smoke of the battle has cleared
away, the verdict will be more valuable, because
more impartial. It will then probably be found
that supporters have been too fulsome and
detractors too acrid, and that the true position
of the composer must be sought between the
extremes. Nevertheless, we think it will be
then admitted on all hands that he deserves
to rank among those who shine as bright
particular stars in the musical world.

The last years of his life were passed in full
contentment at Bayreuth, and when he died
quite suddenly on 13th February 1883 at
Venice, the progress of his coffin through
Austria and Germany was a triumphal procession. In an ivy-covered vault constructed
by himself near his villa, *Wahnfried*, the
remains of the master still are a shrine of
pilgrimage to the increasing thousands that
gather yearly at Bayreuth to listen to his music.
No greater triumph could be vouchsafed to
Wagner's *manes* than the applause which is

tardily bestowed on his works in inimical
Paris.

A man of strong affinities and prejudices, he
more than any other gloried over the disasters
that overtook the French nation, he more than
any other incurred their hatred and prejudice.
That the creations have overcome the repug-
nance inspired by the man is a homage which
his detractors cannot easily explain away.

Though vain (if the consciousness of merit
can be called vanity) and hot tempered, Wagner
was adored by those people who knew him
best. At Bayreuth not a labourer can be
found who will not tell of some proof of his
good-nature, and when his coffin was lowered
into its resting-place the population of a town
shared in the grief of those more nearly affected.

The traits of features are well known : the
keen eye, the Roman nose, and the thin
compressed lips give token of great intelli-
gence ; the long flowing hair reminds one of the
artistic era of Paolo Veronese and Titian, even
if this impression were not heightened by the
velvet cap which in one of his best-known
pictures crowns his head. His figure was of
middle height and strong build, his movements
of that rapid activity which is in keeping with
his abnormal energy. An indefatigable reader,

and a shrewd observer and keen thinker, his literary efforts are of no ordinary merit. In literature, or in fact in any of the walks of life that he might have chosen to take up, it is probable that his vigorous intellect and striking personality would have made its mark.

And now that we have dipped not too deeply into the history, the lives, and struggles of those sons of Music who have emblazoned their names on the scroll of Fame, what more fitting than the final words should be a tribute to the nation whose rugged simplicity, profound philosophy, and poetic ideality have given to the world a Bach, a Beethoven, a Handel, a Mozart, and a Wagner—the grand old Father-land—Germany, out of whose bosom have arisen the glorious pillars supporting the sacred Temple of Music !

THE END

Printed by T. and A. CONSTABLE, Printers to Her Majesty,
at the Edinburgh University Press.

"He who respects his work so highly (and does it reverently) that he cares _little_ what the World thinks of it, is the man about whom the World comes at last to think a good deal"

ImTheStory.com

CPSIA information can be obtained
at www.ICGtesting.com
Printed in the USA
LVHW082258050519
616737LV00016B/275/P

9 781313 405799